FLAG LORE
OF ALL
NATIONS

Whitney Smith, Ph.D.
Director, Flag Research Center

THE MILLBROOK PRESS   BROOKFIELD, CONNECTICUT

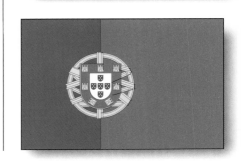

For Vicki

Flag images courtesy of Dream Maker Software.

Library of Congress Cataloging-in-Publication Data
Smith, Whitney.
Flag lore of all nations / Whitney Smith.
p. cm.
Includes bibliographical references and index.
ISBN 0-7613-1753-8 (lib. bdg.) ISBN 0-7613-1899-2 (pbk.)
1. Flags—Juvenile literature. [1. Flags.] I. Title.
CR109 .S63 2001
929.9'2—dc21
00-048973

Published by The Millbrook Press, Inc.
2 Old New Milford Road
Brookfield, Connecticut 06804
www.millbrookpress.com

CONTENTS

INTRODUCTION

Every country in the world has a national flag, and many have secondary national flags for special purposes. Flags are more than just colorful decorations. They announce the presence of a country, for example, at the Olympic Games. They inspire people, proclaim victory, identify government offices and ships, and they also have practical uses. The most important use for most national flags, however, is to define the country and its people. What are they proud of? What are their hopes for the future? What are their politics and their religious beliefs? What are the natural features of the country?

Most national flags tell stories about the country's origins and events that define the nation, although often the stories are not historically accurate. The flag thus expresses a "civil religion" that political groups in the country try to control. This encourages people to support their view of the past, the future, the government and economic system, and relations between different groups of people. The flag of China, for example, defines that country as a united land under the Communist party; the flag of Egypt claims that the country is part of the Arab nation; the pledge to the Stars and Stripes explains that the United States provides "liberty and justice for all." Flag ceremonies, customs, and traditions—including songs, literature, and government propaganda—influence the way people think and act. Belief in the principles of a flag can even make people willing to die while fighting to uphold its meanings.

National flags are only part of the world of vexillology, which is the study of flags. (The word vexillology comes from *vexillum*, which is Latin for flag.) In addition to the national flags shown in this book, every country has many other flags—for its government officials, army and navy, provinces and cities, its religions and political parties, and even flags for businesses and private individuals. Learning about these flags gives us a better understanding of the people who fly them.

Note about this book: All recognized independent countries of the world, including the 189 members of the United Nations, are included in this book. The nonmember countries are Switzerland, Taiwan, and Vatican City. The grid near each flag relates details about how it is used.

National flags are used on land; national ensigns are flown at sea. Usage by private citizens is identified by the word *civil*, usage by the government is identified by the word *state*, and usage by the military is identified by the word *war*. For example, a national flag that is used only on government and military buildings is referred to as a "state and war flag."

Not all countries have all types of flags. Chad, for example, has no ensigns because it is landlocked (enclosed by land). Some countries, including France and Turkey, use a single flag design for all purposes. The type of national flag for each country shown in this book is indicated by a grid pattern, as explained below.

	Use by Private Citizens	*Use by the Government*	*Use by the Military*
Use on Land	CIVIL FLAG	STATE FLAG	WAR FLAG
Use at Sea	CIVIL ENSIGN	STATE ENSIGN	WAR ENSIGN

When a dot appears in any part of the grid pattern, it means that the flag shown is appropriate for that use. For example, ⣰⣋⊢ means that the flag is flown on private and public buildings and on privately owned and government-owned vessels, but not on military installations or ships.

The names of some countries have been changed, including the following:

Burma—see Myanmar
Ivory Coast—see Côte d'Ivoire
St. Christopher—see St. Kitts and Nevis
Western Samoa—see Samoa
Zaire—see Congo, Democratic Republic of the

AFGHANISTAN (af-GAH-nuh-stan): Afghanistan had a great variety of national flags. Every major change in government resulted in the adoption of a different design because each new regime favored its own colors and symbols. The present flag was adopted on January 26, 2002, after the overthrow of the Taliban government. The flag is almost the same as the one used from 1931 until 1973, when Afghanistan was a kingdom. It includes a mosque flanked by flags, a scroll with the name of the country, and the shahadai or "testimony" of the Islamic faith. There is also a wreath of wheat, recalling the crown worn in 1747 by the first Afghan king.

ALBANIA (al-BAY-nee-uh): In the fifteenth century, George Kastrioti, known as Skanderbeg, resisted the Turkish invasion of Albania under a flag of red. It bore a black double-headed eagle, a symbol borrowed from the Byzantine Empire. The same flag was revived in the late nineteenth century by Albanian immigrants in America and Europe. When the independence of Albania was proclaimed on November 28, 1912, the red flag with a black eagle was officially recognized. Different regimes have added special symbols over the eagle heads, but after the fall of communism the original plain design was reestablished on May 22, 1993.

ALGERIA (al-JEER-ee-uh): The crescent and star were considered good-luck symbols in Algeria for many centuries and appeared on certain military flags. In the nineteenth century, France conquered Algeria. Emir Abdelkader, who resisted the French, is said to have used green and white flags. In the 1920s, nationalist leader Messali Hajj created the modern Algerian flag, which was adopted by the National Liberation Front and its army in the 1950s. Finally, Algeria regained its independence on July 3, 1962. The liberation flag then became the new national flag, recalling the heroes of the past century.

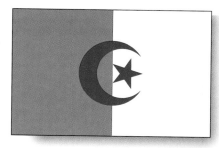

ANDORRA (an-DOR-uh): The date of the first use of the national flag of Andorra is not known, although it is said to have been created in 1866. Many variations of the coat of arms existed until a standardized version was adopted in July 1993 when Andorra joined the United Nations. The arms include symbols of the bishop of Urgel (crosier and miter), the stripes of Foix and of Catalonia, and the cows of Béarn. The colors of those symbols probably suggested the blue-yellow-red of the tricolor (a flag arranged in bands of three colors). The national motto under the shield translates from the Latin as "Strength United Is Stronger."

ANGOLA (an-GOE-luh): Many political groups struggled for control of Angola following the country's independence on November 11, 1975. The Popular Movement for the Liberation of Angola (MPLA), which proved to be the dominant force, used a flag of red and black horizontal stripes and a yellow central star. To create the new national flag a machete (large knife used for farming) and half a cogwheel, representing peasants and workers, were added. The star shows that the nation is under the leadership of the MPLA. The National Union for the Total Independence of Angola, which still controls much of the country, has its own flag.

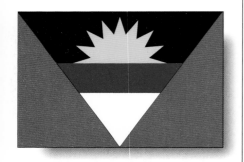

ANTIGUA AND BARBUDA (an-TEE-guh and bar-BOO-duh): Reginald Samuel was the winner in a competition for a national flag at the time Antigua and Barbuda achieved local self-government on February 27, 1967. The people (black), the sea (blue), the beaches (white), and the sun (yellow) were reflected in his design. The red background suggests a dynamic people working out their future; the V-shape stands for victory. Antigua and Barbuda retained the same flag when it became independent on November 1, 1981.

ARGENTINA (ahr-jen-TEE-nuh): In May 1810, the Patriots who established a local government in Argentina, then under Spanish rule, wore blue cockades (badges). The patron saint of the country, the Virgin of Luján, was dressed in blue and white. One or both of these may have influenced the choice of colors for the first Argentine national flag, adopted on February 12, 1812. The blue-white-blue flag was decorated with a golden sun on February 25, 1818. That symbol recalled the brilliant "Sun of May" that had shone through clouds in 1810, when the Spanish governor ceded control to the Patriots. Argentina has used the flag ever since.

ARMENIA (ahr-MEE-nee-uh): The first national flag for Armenia was designed in the late nineteenth century, before it obtained its independence from Russia. On May 28, 1918, freedom was finally achieved, and on August 1 a new red-blue-orange flag was recognized. The colors stood for the blood shed for Armenia by its people, their eternal homeland, and for courage and work. From 1921 until 1990, when Armenia was part of the Soviet Union, its tricolor was not forgotten by Armenians. It was readopted on August 24, 1990, when the local parliament announced its intention to proclaim independence for Armenia again.

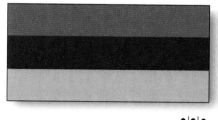

AUSTRALIA (aw-STRALE-yuh): Six British colonies united on January 1, 1901, to form the new Commonwealth of Australia. A contest was held for a national flag, but it was not until May 22, 1909, that the final design became official. The Union Jack (state flag of the United Kingdom) showed that Australia was still under British rule; the large star represented the Commonwealth (the union of the states of Australia). At the fly end (the outer or loose end of the flag), the stars of the Southern Cross constellation symbolized the geographical position of Australia. Since World War II many Australians have come to feel that a distinctive new flag should be created. None of the design proposals submitted has yet found majority approval, however.

AUSTRIA (AWS-tree-uh): The basic design of the Austrian shield, which forms the basis for the nation's red-white-red flag, dates from at least the year 1230. Legend attributes the flag to a battle that occurred a century earlier during the Crusades (Christian expeditions to win the Holy Land from the Muslims). When Austria became a great empire in the Middle Ages, the imperial symbol—a black eagle on a yellow field—was used as a flag. In 1919, Austria was reduced to its present borders and the red and white tribar (flag with three stripes) became the national flag. The eagle still appears, but only on government and other official flags.

AZERBAIJAN (ah-zer-bie-JAHN): Ali Bay Huseynzada, the leading nationalist of Azerbaijan, created its modern national flag. The colors of that tricolor stood for the Turkic people (blue), their Islamic faith (green), and the commitment to modernization (red). In the center of the flag was the traditional Muslim star and crescent. The eight points stood for the eight Turkic peoples, including the Azerbaijanis. This flag was used from 1918 to 1920, when Azerbaijan was independent, and it was revived on February 5, 1991. After the fall of the Soviet Union, independence for Azerbaijan under this flag was proclaimed on August 30, 1991.

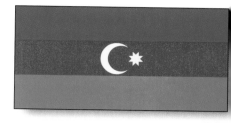

BAHAMAS (buh-HA-muz): A distinctive shade of aquamarine was chosen for the stripes of the new national flag of the Bahamas at the time of independence from Great Britain on July 10, 1973. Those stripes represent the beautiful waters surrounding the islands, while the yellow stripe suggests the sand and other resources that attract tourists. The people of the islands and their strength are reflected in the black triangle. Prior to independence, a competition was held to design a new flag, but nobody is credited with the result.

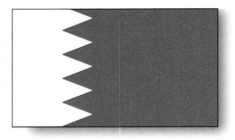

BAHRAIN (bah-RANE): Since at least the beginning of the nineteenth century, many small Arab states in the Arabian Gulf have displayed flags of white and red, traditional local symbols of peace and war. The modern national flag of Bahrain may date from the nineteenth century, but it only became official in 1933 and was slightly modified in 1972. No changes were made in the national flag of the country at the time of its independence from Britain on August 15, 1971. On February 20, 2002, Bahrain became a kingdom and the number of zigzags in the flag was reduced to five, corresponding to the five obligations of the faithful Muslim.

BANGLADESH (bahn-gluh-DESH): When the people in East Pakistan began to fight for their independence, they chose a flag of green to symbolize their Islamic faith. In the center was a red disk standing for the blood shed in the liberation struggle. Placed on the disk was a silhouette map of their country, Bangladesh, in yellow. After freedom was achieved the national flag was modified on January 25, 1972; the disk was shifted toward the hoist (the attached edge of the flag), and the map was eliminated.

BARBADOS (bahr-BAY-dose): Local artist Grantley Prescod was the winner in a flag design competition held just before the proclamation of independence for Barbados on November 30, 1966. He proposed stripes of blue representing sea and sky, with a yellow stripe between them for the island's sand. In the center of the flag he added a trident (three-pronged spear) head in black as a distinctive symbol. Under British colonial rule, the flag badge of Barbados had shown a king holding a trident, the symbol traditionally associated with Poseidon/Neptune, the god of the ocean.

BELARUS (byell-uh-ROOS): The country known as the Byelorussian Soviet Socialist Republic became independent in 1991 and readopted a flag that had been used following World War I. On June 7, 1995, however, the Soviet-era flag was reestablished minus its hammer, sickle, and star. It has a horizontal stripe of red over light green, standing for communism and the forests of the country. At the hoist is a white vertical stripe with the red embroidery pattern found in traditional Belorussian clothing. The colors correspond to the name of the country—"White Russia." The flag had originally been adopted in 1951 under Soviet rule.

BELGIUM (BEL-jum): Use of the colors black, yellow, and red in the flag of Belgium is based on the shield of Brabant, one of the Belgian provinces. The shield dates from the early thirteenth century and features a golden lion with red tongue and claws on a black background. In 1787, Belgian opposition to Austrian rule was expressed by wearing a black-yellow-red cockade. In 1830 the movement for independence was begun with the same cockade, and on January 23, 1831, the national flag was adopted. Some early flags had horizontal stripes, but since 1838 vertical stripes have been standard.

BELIZE (buh-LEEZ): The movement for independence began in 1950, as symbolized by the fifty leaves surrounding the coat of arms. Dating from 1819, the arms shows some of the men and tools involved in the lumber industry, an important part of the national economy. A blue flag with the arms in the center was first used by the People's United party. In anticipation of independence on September 21, 1981, red stripes were added at the top and bottom of the flag to symbolize the United Democratic party. The Latin motto on the coat of arms translates to "I Flourish in the Shade."

16

BENIN (buh-NEEN): The national flag of Dahomey, adopted on November 16, 1959, featured stripes in red, yellow, and green—the pan-African colors (see *Mali*). No change was made at independence on August 1, 1960. However, on December 1, 1975, the name of the country was changed to Benin and its flag was altered. When the nation's Marxist regime ended, the original flag was restored on August 1, 1990, although the country's name remained the same. The colors symbolize the savannas of the north (yellow) and the palm groves of the south (green); red is for those who died defending the homeland.

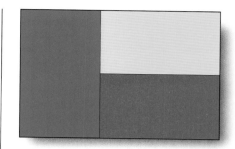

BHUTAN (boo-TAN): The yellow of the national flag is a symbol of the power of the king. The orange triangle has a religious significance for Buddhists, while the white is for purity and loyalty. In its native language, the name of Bhutan translates as "Land of the Thunder Dragon," and local people believe that they can hear the voice of dragons in the mountains. The jewels in the claws of the dragon stand for the wealth of the nation and its national perfection. The dragon flag had long been in use before the current version was established in 1971.

17

BOLIVIA (buh-LIV-ee-uh): The first national flag of Bolivia was adopted on August 17, 1825, soon after independence. A year later the design was altered, and on November 5, 1851, the basic red-yellow-green version in use today was established. Red stands for the valor of the army, yellow for mineral resources, and green for the fertility of the land. The coat of arms shows a typical Bolivian landscape with a mountain, alpaca, breadfruit tree, wheat sheaf, and sun. The shield bears stars for the provinces and is surrounded by flags and a condor, the national bird.

BOSNIA AND HERZEGOVINA (BOZ-nee-uh and hurt-suh-goe-VEE-nuh): Independence for Bosnia was achieved on March 3, 1992, under its Communist-era flag. Two months later a new national flag was adopted, but the design was rejected by Bosnian Serbs and Croats. After years of civil war, peace settlements were signed in Dayton, Ohio, that required Bosnia to adopt a new national flag. When no agreement could be reached, United Nations officials imposed a flag on the country. Its triangle suggests the shape of Bosnia, while the blue and yellow colors recall the flag of Europe. The stars have no official symbolism.

BOTSWANA (botch-WAH-nuh): Because the country is very arid, rain is important for people in Botswana. Therefore, the blue of its national flag refers to life-giving water, and the word *pula* (rain) is the motto of the country. The black-and-white stripes of the flag were chosen expressly to symbolize racial cooperation between Caucasians and native Africans at a time when neighboring South Africa was under the apartheid regime, which discriminated against blacks. The zebra was chosen as the national animal of Botswana for the same reason. The flag was hoisted at the time of national independence on September 30, 1966.

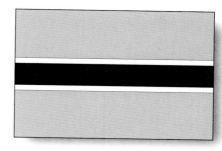

BRAZIL (bruh-ZIL): The rich jungles and fields of the country are symbolized by the green of the national flag, while its mineral wealth is reflected in the yellow diamond. The colors were chosen by the wife of the Brazilian king at the time of independence in 1822. In 1889 the country became a republic and replaced the royal coat of arms on the flag with a blue disk bearing a motto that translates as "Order and Progress." Stars for each of the states were arranged in constellations, with one star standing for the national territories. The newest stars were added to the flag on May 12, 1992.

BRUNEI (broo-NIE): The original flag of Brunei was plain yellow, but in 1906 stripes of black and white were added for the chief ministers of the sultan. The flag was again modified in September 1959, when a new constitution was introduced, by the addition of the Brunei coat of arms. It includes the name of the country and the motto "Always Render Service by the Guidance of God." There is a crescent for Islam and hands symbolizing peace, prosperity, and well-being. At the top of the arms are the royal umbrella and a small flag. Minor changes were made in the flag on January 1, 1984, at independence.

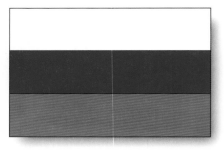

BULGARIA (bul-GARE-ee-uh): On April 16, 1879, the white-green-red Bulgarian tricolor was officially recognized, following the war in 1878 through which the country gained its independence. The colors were chosen to honor Russia, the country's most important ally. The new tricolor is the same as the Russian flag except that the central stripe is green. The red is interpreted as standing for military courage and struggle, while the white is for love, peace, and freedom. Green suggests the agricultural wealth of Bulgaria. The current flag dates from November 27, 1990, when Communist symbols previously in use were omitted from the white stripe.

BURKINA FASO (bur-KEE-nuh FAH-soe): The Republic of Upper Volta, formerly a French colony, became independent on December 9, 1959, under a black-white-red horizontally striped flag. After a revolution took place in 1983, the new government changed the country's name and national symbols on August 4, 1984. Hope and abundance are symbolized by green; revolutionary struggle by red. The yellow star brings attention to national mineral wealth. The new name of the country translates as "Land of the Righteous."

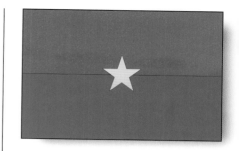

BURUNDI (boo-ROON-dee): The basic design of the national flag was established just prior to independence on July 1, 1962. The diagonal cross (called a saltire in heraldry) and central disk are white, referring to peace. Red is for the independence struggle, and green stands for the people's belief in future development. In the center of the flag are red stars fimbriated (narrowly bordered) in green, which hint at the national motto—"Unity, Work, Progress." This three-star design was originally established after Burundi became a republic and was most recently modified on September 27, 1982.

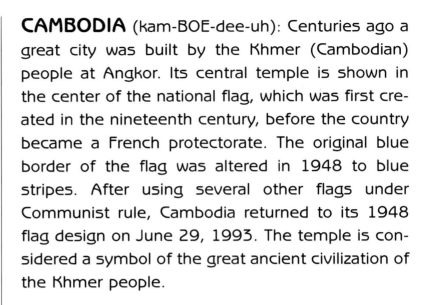

CAMBODIA (kam-BOE-dee-uh): Centuries ago a great city was built by the Khmer (Cambodian) people at Angkor. Its central temple is shown in the center of the national flag, which was first created in the nineteenth century, before the country became a French protectorate. The original blue border of the flag was altered in 1948 to blue stripes. After using several other flags under Communist rule, Cambodia returned to its 1948 flag design on June 29, 1993. The temple is considered a symbol of the great ancient civilization of the Khmer people.

CAMEROON (kam-uh-ROON): The African Democratic Rally (see *Mali*), a political party in Cameroon, used green, yellow, and red as its colors. A vertically striped flag in those colors—similar to the French tricolor used by the power administering the country—was adopted by Cameroon on October 29, 1957. Later some changes were made in the symbols on the stripes, most recently on May 20, 1975. To show national unity, today there is a single yellow star. Green recalls the rich lands of the south, while yellow is for the savannas of the north. Red stands for national sovereignty and for unity between north and south.

CANADA (KAN-uh-duh): As Canada approached the centennial of national confederation in 1967, Prime Minister Lester B. Pearson decided that there should be a distinctive Canadian national flag. Despite considerable opposition and after long debate, Parliament adopted the present design, which became effective on February 15, 1965. The red and white were chosen because they were already considered to be the Canadian national colors, based on the national coat of arms granted in 1921. The red stood for the sacrifice that Canadians had made during World War I. The maple leaf has been widely used as a Canadian symbol since at least 1867.

CAPE VERDE (kape vurd): A single political party dominated Cape Verde from the time of its independence until multiparty elections took place in 1991. The opposition Movement for Democracy won those elections and created a new national flag on September 25, 1992. The stars stand for the ten islands that constitute the country. Blue and white are Portuguese colors, while red, white, and blue are American colors; Cape Verde has close links to both countries. The blue of the flag stands for the Atlantic Ocean, white is for peace, and red expresses national determination to develop the country.

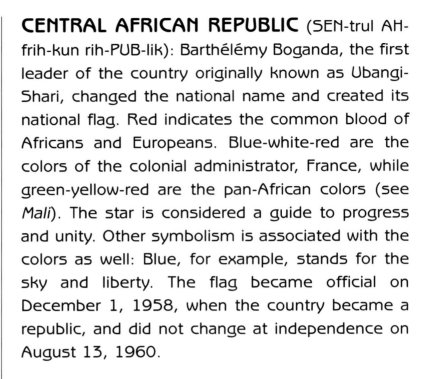

CENTRAL AFRICAN REPUBLIC (SEN-trul AH-frih-kun rih-PUB-lik): Barthélémy Boganda, the first leader of the country originally known as Ubangi-Shari, changed the national name and created its national flag. Red indicates the common blood of Africans and Europeans. Blue-white-red are the colors of the colonial administrator, France, while green-yellow-red are the pan-African colors (see *Mali*). The star is considered a guide to progress and unity. Other symbolism is associated with the colors as well: Blue, for example, stands for the sky and liberty. The flag became official on December 1, 1958, when the country became a republic, and did not change at independence on August 13, 1960.

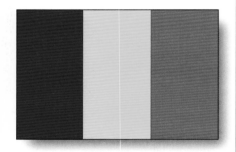

CHAD (chad): France was the colonial ruler of most West African territories for many decades before it introduced local self-government. Many of the national flags for these countries, including the flag of Chad, were adopted quickly and with few historical connections. The inspiration for the three equal vertical stripes used by Chad and several other countries was the famous tricolor of France. Its central stripe was changed to yellow (for the sun) in the flag of Chad, which became official on November 6, 1959. Blue refers to the sky and hope, while red is for national unity.

CHILE (CHIL-ee): The first symbols of independence in Chile were cockades (badges), worn by patriots in the early nineteenth century. The first known cockade was blue-white-yellow, followed by red-white-blue. Finally, on October 18, 1817, the national flag was established in the form still used today. The design was based on the American Stars and Stripes, although the colors had previously been used by Indians in Chile. Red is for the blood of those who died for the country, white for the snow of the Andes Mountains, and blue for the sky. The star is "a guide on the path of progress and honor."

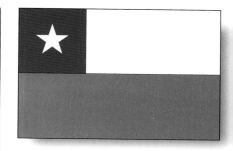

CHINA (CHIE-nuh): Five has always been considered a lucky number in China: There are ancient references to the Five Elements, Five Rulers, etc. There are also five traditional ethnic groups in the country—the Han (or Chinese), the Manchu, the Mongols, the Tibetans, and the Hui (or Muslims) of Sinkiang. When the People's Republic of China was established on October 1, 1949, the small stars on its flag were said to stand for its four social classes, and the large star represented the Chinese Communist party. Red is the traditional color of the Han and the Communists.

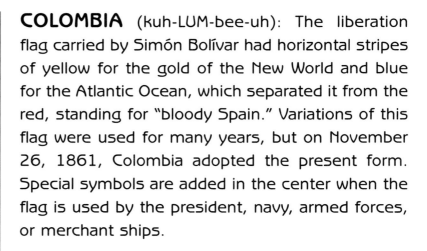

COLOMBIA (kuh-LUM-bee-uh): The liberation flag carried by Simón Bolívar had horizontal stripes of yellow for the gold of the New World and blue for the Atlantic Ocean, which separated it from the red, standing for "bloody Spain." Variations of this flag were used for many years, but on November 26, 1861, Colombia adopted the present form. Special symbols are added in the center when the flag is used by the president, navy, armed forces, or merchant ships.

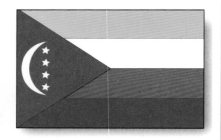

COMOROS (KAH-muh-roze): Since 1975 when the country became independent, Comoros has had six different national flags. All of these flags, however, have included the color green and the star and crescent emblem, which are also used by many other Muslim countries. The four stars stand for the islands of Grande-Comore, Anjouan, and Mwéli, as well as the French-controlled island of Mayotte, which is claimed by Comoros. The present flag was adopted on December 23, 2001, following a referendum that established a new constitution. The four stripes of the flag show that the islands have local self-government.

CONGO (KAHN-goe), **DEMOCRATIC REPUB-LIC OF THE**: The former Belgian Congo (originally the Congo Free State) became independent on June 30, 1960. It used the flag first established in 1877 for the Free State—a yellow star in the center of a blue background—but added six yellow stars along the hoist to symbolize the provinces of the country. Other flags were used over the years until May 17, 1997. A new revolutionary government then revived the original flag, even though the number of provinces in the country had changed. The country was known as Zaire from 1971 to 1997.

CONGO (KAHN-goe), **REPUBLIC OF THE**: On September 15, 1959, the first flag of the Congo was adopted, consisting of vertical stripes of green, yellow, and red. The first two colors stood for agriculture and friendship; the symbolism of the red was not known. A new flag was later created by a Marxist government, but on June 10, 1991, the original flag was reestablished. The use of three stripes was undoubtedly influenced by the French tricolor and the three pan-African colors (red, yellow, and green), which were used by many countries at the time the Congo adopted its flag (see *Mali*). The Republic of the Congo is also known as Congo-Brazzaville because Brazzaville is the country's capital.

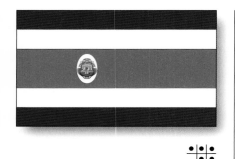

COSTA RICA (KAWS-tuh REE-kuh): Like the other former members of the United Provinces of the Center of America, Costa Rica adopted a national flag of blue and white when it separated and became independent. On September 29, 1848, however, a stripe of red was added to the center of the flag at the suggestion of the wife of President José María Castro Madriz. The new symbol was said to stand for the sun of independence and the advancement of civilization. The coat of arms of Costa Rica that appears on the flag features five volcanoes and seven stars for the country's seven provinces.

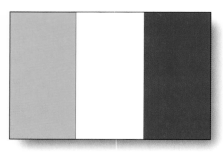

CÔTE D'IVOIRE (kote dee-VWAR): When France began to end its African colonial empire in the late 1950s, new flags were adopted by the new republics that developed. In many cases the flags resembled the French tricolor. Côte d'Ivoire created its flag on December 3, 1959, and became independent on August 7 of the following year. The three stripes of the flag stand for the three words in the national motto—"Unity, Discipline, Labor." The colors refer to the savannas of the north and the forests of the south, while white stands for unity and purity. The country's name translates as "Ivory Coast" in English.

CROATIA (kroe-AY-shuh): The first use of a red-white-blue horizontal tricolor flag by Croatia occurred during the revolution of 1848. The colors were chosen to symbolize Slavic unity. The Croatian tricolor was suppressed while the country was part of Yugoslavia from 1918 to 1941. The fascist Independent State of Croatia, which existed from 1941 to 1945, employed this flag with other symbols added. The same colors were used by the Communist regime of 1946–1990 with a large central red star. The current design was adopted on December 22, 1990, following Croatian independence. The traditional checkered shield of Croatia is surmounted by five historic shields from its various parts: From left to right these emblems stand for old Croatia, Dubrovnik (Ragusa), Dalmatia, Istria, and Slavonia.

CUBA (KYOO-buh): The United States flag was the inspiration for the design of the Cuban flag, which dates from 1850. The three stripes of blue are for the military districts then existing in the Spanish-ruled island of Cuba; the two white stripes are for purity. The red triangle symbolizes strength, while the star stands for independence. Americans defeated the Spanish during their war in 1898, but Cuba was not given its freedom until May 20, 1902. On that day its flag was hoisted for the first time officially. No change was made when Fidel Castro introduced his Communist regime in Cuba fifty years later.

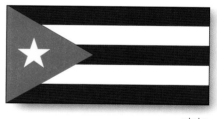

29

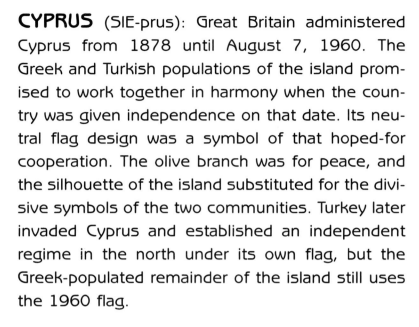

CYPRUS (SIE-prus): Great Britain administered Cyprus from 1878 until August 7, 1960. The Greek and Turkish populations of the island promised to work together in harmony when the country was given independence on that date. Its neutral flag design was a symbol of that hoped-for cooperation. The olive branch was for peace, and the silhouette of the island substituted for the divisive symbols of the two communities. Turkey later invaded Cyprus and established an independent regime in the north under its own flag, but the Greek-populated remainder of the island still uses the 1960 flag.

CZECH REPUBLIC (chek rih-PUH-blik): The traditional national colors of the Czech people were white and red, based on the shield of Bohemia, which is red with a white double-tailed lion. When Czechoslovakia obtained its independence in 1918, the first national flag adopted was simply white over red stripes. In 1920, however, a blue triangle was added at the hoist because blue was found in the heraldic symbols of Slovakia and Ruthenia, the other parts of the new republic. The flag of Czechoslovakia was revived in 1945, and in 1993, when Slovakia seceded (withdrew), it was retained by the new Czech Republic.

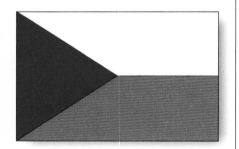

DENMARK (DEN-mahrk): According to legend, the flag of Denmark fell from the sky on June 15, 1219, during a battle between King Valdemar II of Denmark and the pagan Estonians. The real origin of the flag is not known. The red background probably was taken from the Imperial War Flag of the Holy Roman Empire, and the cross symbolizes Christianity. Despite centuries of use, the "Dannebrog" did not legally become a national flag available to all the people until 1854, after the Danes fought a war with Prussia.

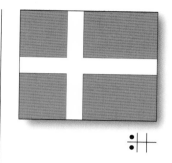

DJIBOUTI (juh-BOO-tee): The colors green and light blue of the Djibouti flag are associated with two local ethnic groups, the Afars and the Issas. White indicates peace, while red is for independence. The triangle stands for equality, and the star is for unity. The flag was first hoisted when independence was achieved on June 27, 1977. A similar flag had been used by the Liberation Front of the Coast of the Somalis (the previous name for the territory) prior to independence from French colonial rule. The same light blue color appears in the flag of neighboring Somalia.

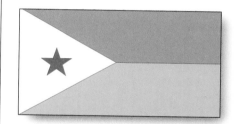

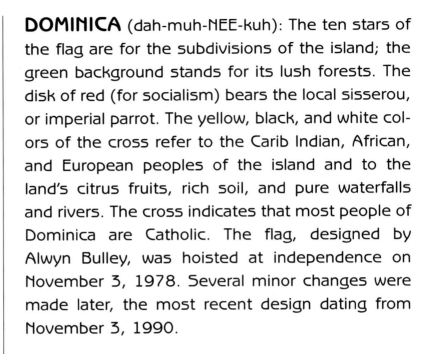

DOMINICA (dah-muh-NEE-kuh): The ten stars of the flag are for the subdivisions of the island; the green background stands for its lush forests. The disk of red (for socialism) bears the local sisserou, or imperial parrot. The yellow, black, and white colors of the cross refer to the Carib Indian, African, and European peoples of the island and to the land's citrus fruits, rich soil, and pure waterfalls and rivers. The cross indicates that most people of Dominica are Catholic. The flag, designed by Alwyn Bulley, was hoisted at independence on November 3, 1978. Several minor changes were made later, the most recent design dating from November 3, 1990.

DOMINICAN REPUBLIC (duh-MIH-nih-kuhn rih-PUH-blik): La Trinitaria, the revolutionary group that sought independence for the Spanish-speaking part of Haiti in 1844, added a white cross to the blue and red horizontally striped national flag of Haiti. When that movement brought the Dominican Republic to independence, the constitution of November 6, 1844, defined the flag more precisely. The blue and red squares in the corners were alternated, and the coat of arms of the country was added at the center of the cross. It includes the national motto "God, Fatherland, Liberty" in Spanish, a Bible, a small gold cross, the name of the country, draped flags, and a wreath of laurel and palm.

ECUADOR (EH-kwuh-dor): Like its neighbors—Colombia and Venezuela—with whom it was once united, Ecuador uses a tricolor of yellow-blue-red dating from the early nineteenth century. The national coat of arms in the center of the flag, as used by the government, features a condor and a scene with a river and Mount Chimborazo. The flag was officially adopted on November 7, 1900.

EGYPT (EE-jipt): When army officers overthrew the monarchy in Egypt in 1952, they rallied under the new Arab Liberation Flag of red, white, and black stripes that they had created. The colors stood for their revolution, the bright future of the country, and the dark days of the past. In 1958 this design was adopted as a national flag with two green stars to symbolize Egypt's union with Syria. The central emblem was changed to a gold hawk in 1972. The current design, which dates from October 4, 1984, shows the gold eagle of the twelfth-century Muslim leader Saladin, who built a palace in Cairo.

EL SALVADOR (el SAL-vuh-dor): The Central American states proclaimed their independence as a federation on September 15, 1821, but soon became part of Mexico. When independence was again established two years later, the new national flag adopted had blue-white-blue horizontal stripes. This had originally been used by Colonel Manuel José Arce of El Salvador in 1822, based on a similar flag displayed in the Caribbean in 1818, when Argentina was promoting the independence of Spanish colonies. El Salvador used the tribar flag until 1865 and then readopted it on September 15, 1912. With minor modifications it is still in use today.

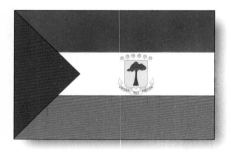

EQUATORIAL GUINEA (ee-kwuh-TOR-ee-ul GIH-nee): The blood of martyrs (red), peace (white), and agriculture (green) are the meanings of the stripes in the national flag of Equatorial Guinea, first used at independence on October 12, 1968. The blue triangle refers to the ocean because the country consists of several islands and a coastal territory on mainland Africa. The coat of arms, created soon after independence, was reestablished on August 21, 1979, after a dictator was overthrown. The arms includes a god tree (a symbol used under Spanish rule), the Spanish motto "Unity, Peace, Justice," and gold stars for the subdivisions of the country.

ERITREA (er-uh-TREE-uh): The national flag was first officially hoisted at the proclamation of independence on May 24, 1993, and was slightly modified in 1995. The green stands for agriculture, and the blue for maritime resources. The red recalls the bloody thirty-year battle for freedom, and the yellow of the olive wreath and branches is for mineral resources. The original flag of Eritrea had been used from 1952 until 1958: It had a background of light blue (for the United Nations flag) and the same emblem found in the modern flag, but in green instead of yellow. Eritrea was part of Ethiopia for years.

ESTONIA (eh-STOE-nee-uh): The stripes of the national flag stand for the sky (blue), the soil (black), and the desire for freedom (white). The flag was dedicated on June 4, 1884, by Vironia, a student organization in Estonia, then part of the Russian Empire. It served as the national flag of Estonia during its period of independence from 1918 until 1940. The flag was legalized again in 1988, and two years later, when Estonia ceased to be part of the Soviet Union, its tricolor was recognized as the national flag of an independent country.

ETHIOPIA (ee-thee-OE-pee-uh): The first national flag of Ethiopia was created on October 6, 1897. Like the present flag, it had horizontal stripes of green-yellow-red, although the color order was reversed. In the center was the initial letter of the king's name. Different variations of that flag were used over the following century, except for the years when Ethiopia was occupied by Italy. Red, yellow, and green are the pan-African colors (see *Mali*) found in many flags created in the late 1950s and 1960s, inspired in part by their use in Ethiopia, which is the continent's oldest independent nation. Ethiopia's present flag was adopted in 1996 after many years of Communist rule. The blue disk is for peace, the yellow-rayed star for unity, hope, equality, and justice.

FIJI (FEE-jee): As a British colony, Fiji used a dark blue flag with the Union Jack, or flag of the United Kingdom, in the canton (upper corner of the flag), and its own coat of arms at the center of the fly end. When Fiji became independent on October 10, 1970, a few modifications were made in the flag: Most strikingly, the background was changed from dark blue to light blue. The shield only of the coat of arms now appears; it contains the cross of St. George of England as well as an English lion holding a cacao pod. It also features sugarcane, a coconut palm, bananas, and a dove with an olive branch.

FINLAND (FIN-luhnd): Many proposals for a Finnish flag were made when the country was under Russian rule. In 1862, Zachris Topelius suggested a flag of white for snow and a cross of blue for the country's lakes; the general design resembled those of other Nordic countries. In 1917, Finland obtained its independence and considered several national flags, including some in blue and white and others in red and yellow, the colors of its coat of arms. The basic design by Topelius was adopted in 1918 with the shade of blue changing from light to dark in 1978. As used by the government the cross has the Finnish arms in the center, showing a lion and nine roses.

FRANCE (frants): The famous tricolor, which has inspired many national flags around the world, was adopted by France in 1790 as a naval jack (a small flag flown by a ship) and revised to its present form in 1794. The colors were first used in 1789 at the beginning of the French Revolution: White was the Bourbon royal color, while blue and red were used by the city of Paris. As the "Colors of Liberty" these three had already appeared in the Dutch and American flags. The plain white flag was reestablished in France from 1815 to 1830, but since that time the tricolor has symbolized France under every constitution and government.

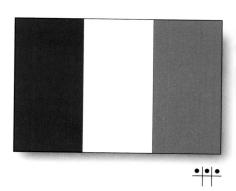

37

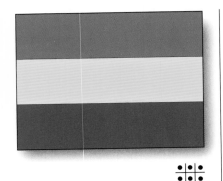

GABON (gah-BONE): On June 29, 1959, Gabon adopted a horizontally striped flag of green, yellow, and blue with the French tricolor in the canton; the yellow stripe was narrower than the others. The present flag dates from August 9, 1960, when Gabon became independent. The equator, which runs through the land, is suggested by the yellow stripe of its flag. Blue is for the South Atlantic Ocean, which runs along the Gabon coast. Green is for the rich forests that provide the country with substantial income. Unlike many former French colonies, Gabon did not choose a vertical tricolor, and it did not include red as part of its flag.

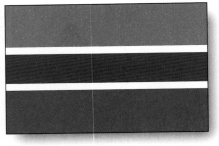

THE GAMBIA (GAM-bee-uh): The former British colony, which includes narrow strips of land on both sides of the Gambia River, based its name and flag on that important natural feature. Blue is for the river itself, red stands for the position of the country in the equatorial region of Africa, while green emphasizes that the people depend on agriculture for food and for export. The white fimbriations (narrow stripes) stand for unity and peace in this design, which became official on February 18, 1965, at the time of Gambian independence. The flag was designed by L. Thomasi.

GEORGIA (JOR-juh): The most famous ruler of Georgia in the Middle Ages was Queen Tamara. Her flag is supposed to have been white with a dark-red cross and a star. Many subsequent flags in the various kingdoms into which Georgia was divided before becoming part of Russia had the same colors. When independence was proclaimed in 1918, the new national flag was cherry red with black and white stripes in the canton, suggesting difficult times in the past and hope for the future. From 1921 until 1991, Georgia was part of the Soviet Union, but the old flag was readopted on November 14, 1990.

GERMANY (JUR-muh-nee): In the early nineteenth century German nationalists began to demonstrate for the unification of the country under a democratic government. Hopes were high when the German Confederation was founded in 1848. Its flag was a horizontal tricolor of black-red-yellow, based on colors from the uniforms of military and student organizations. Use of the flag ended in 1852, and many decades followed under the black-white-red horizontal tricolor of the German Empire. The black-red-yellow flag was revived by the Weimar Republic in 1919 and again in 1945 with the defeat of the Nazis, whose flags had flown from 1933 to the end of World War II. The German Democratic Republic (East Germany) had a flag of its own from 1959 to 1990.

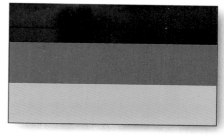

GHANA (GAH-nuh): The black "lodestar of African freedom" appears on a flag of red (for the independence struggle), yellow (for national wealth), and green (for farms and forests). This flag was first hoisted when the former Gold Coast, a British colony, became independent on March 6, 1957. The political organization responsible for ending colonial rule, the Convention People's party, had used a horizontal flag of red-white-green on which the national flag was based. Between 1964 and 1966 the Convention People's party was the sole political party in Ghana, and the national flag had a central stripe of white instead of yellow.

GREECE (grees): In their long struggle against Turkish occupation of their country, Christian Greeks often flew flags of blue and white and used the cross as a symbol. A national flag was adopted in March 1822, after freedom was gained for part of the country, which incorporated both those Christian emblems. The nine stripes of the new flag corresponded to the nine syllables in the Greek phrase translated as "Freedom or Death," which had been used as a battle cry. Since 1970, the blue of the flag has been darker than that previously used, and since 1978 the alternate national flag (blue with a cross but without stripes) is no longer official.

GRENADA (gruh-NAY-duh): The distinctive new national flag of Grenada was hoisted at the time of national independence on February 7, 1974. It has stars representing the subdivisions of the country and a border of red for unity and harmony. Yellow is for wisdom and sunshine; green for agriculture. A nutmeg near the hoist recalls that this and similar spices are an important source of revenue for the island. From 1967 to 1974, when Grenada had only local self-government, there was a different flag. Its horizontal stripes were blue, yellow, and green; in the center it included a nutmeg.

GUATEMALA (gwah-tuh-MAH-luh): The basic design of the national flag was established on November 18, 1871. Like other Central American countries, Guatemala uses stripes of blue-white-blue, but in this case they are vertical instead of horizontal and light blue instead of dark. The coat of arms is also unique: In the center is a quetzal, a bird that cannot live in captivity and therefore symbolizes freedom. The scroll it rests on gives the date of independence of Central America, September 15, 1821. A wreath, rifles, and sabers complete the design. The current versions of the arms and flag date from December 26, 1997.

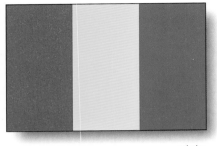

GUINEA (GIH-nee): The Democratic Party of Guinea (PDG), the country's leading political organization, used the pan-African colors red, yellow, and green (see *Mali*) in rallying people in favor of more self-government in what was then a French colony. When voters rejected the new constitution proposed by France in October 1958, Guinea became independent within a week. The new national flag was adopted on November 10, incorporating the PDG colors in the vertical tricolor pattern long used by France. Red is for labor and sacrifice, yellow for justice and mineral wealth, green for agricultural labor and solidarity. Other African nations soon chose the same flag colors.

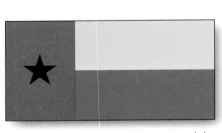

GUINEA-BISSAU (GIH-nee-bih-SOW): Independence for the centuries-old Portuguese colony of Guinea was obtained through a revolutionary struggle led by the African Party for the Independence of Guinea and Cape Verde (PAIGC). Its flag had horizontal stripes of yellow for labor and green for agriculture. At the hoist was a red vertical stripe bearing a black star symbolizing freedom and dignity for the African people. The yellow, green, and red are considered pan-African colors (see *Mali*). It became the national flag when independence was proclaimed on September 24, 1973. The party flag of the PAIGC also bore its initials below the star, but they were not included in the national flag.

GUYANA (guy-AH-nuh): In 1960 the author of this book sent a flag design to Prime Minister Cheddi Jagan of British Guiana, who added it to the many other proposals received. When the British finally agreed to independence for their colony, the author's flag design was slightly modified. Parliament officially adopted it, and when Guyana became independent on May 26, 1966, the flag was first officially raised. Green stands for the jungles and fields, white for the many rivers of Guyana; black is for perseverance, and red for nation building. The golden arrowhead symbolizes a thrust forward to a golden future for the country and recalls the original Indian inhabitants of Guyana.

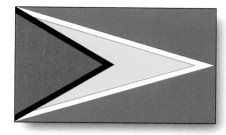

HAITI (HAY-tee): The tricolor of France was the only flag in Haiti when slaves there rose in revolt against their white masters. In 1803 the flag's white stripe was removed, leaving a blue stripe to symbolize Haitian blacks and a red stripe for the mulattoes. In 1840 the stripes were changed from vertical to horizontal and the national coat of arms was added in the center of the flag. These arms show a palm tree, crossed flags, cannon and other weapons, and the national motto—"Union Makes Strength." The flag was most recently adopted on February 25, 1986.

43

HONDURAS (hahn-DUHR-us): On July 1, 1823, the United Provinces of the Center of America became an independent country under a national flag of blue-white-blue with a coat of arms in the center. Eventually Honduras and the other four member countries seceded and created their own flags. Honduras chose its flag on February 16, 1866, based on the Central American triband, which it had continued to use after independence on November 5, 1838. In the center of the blue and white stripes five blue stars were added, which referred to Honduras and its former associates—El Salvador, Nicaragua, Costa Rica, and Guatemala.

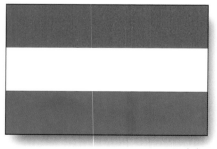

HUNGARY (HUN-guh-ree): The simple Hungarian tricolor, officially adopted on October 1, 1957, replaced earlier versions of the national flag, which had displayed various coats of arms in the center. Red is seen as a reminder of blood shed in past battles, white suggests the rivers of Hungary, and green is for its mountains. Those three colors were found in the old Hungarian coat of arms—a red shield with three green hills at the bottom from which a white double-barred cross rose. The tricolor had been created in the early nineteenth century and was first officially recognized in 1848.

ICELAND (ISE-luhnd): For many centuries Iceland was under the rule of Denmark and had no flag of its own. In the late nineteenth century the Icelandic people came to desire a national flag of their own, but the Danish king resisted. A Scandinavian-type cross design was finally approved in 1915 that combined the traditional blue and white of Iceland and the red and white of the Danish flag. On June 17, 1944, the country became an independent republic, and its parliament changed the blue to a darker shade.

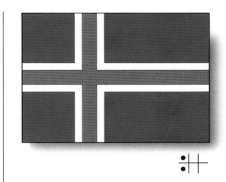

INDIA (IN-dee-uh): In 1921, a national flag for India with white-red-green stripes was suggested by a student, Pinglay Venkayya. Lala Hans Raj Sondhi suggested adding the traditional Indian spinning wheel in the center. In August 1931, the design was approved by the dominant Congress party; it included the current arrangement of stripes and a change from the original red to orange. When India finally became independent on August 15, 1947, the symbol was altered to the historic wheel of Asoka, an ancient Indian emperor. The colors stand for courage and sacrifice (orange), peace and truth (white), and faith and chivalry (green).

INDONESIA (in-duh-NEE-zhuh): In the late thirteenth century the Majapahit Empire in the East Indies used flags of red and white, although there was no national flag of the modern type. In 1922, those colors were adopted by the Indonesian Union, a student organization, when the country was under Dutch colonial rule. The Nationalist party, which fought against colonialism, also used this flag. Independence from the Netherlands was proclaimed on August 17, 1945, and the red and white bicolor became the national flag of Indonesia. Separate states with flags of their own existed in parts of Indonesia until the central government was able to extend its authority throughout the islands.

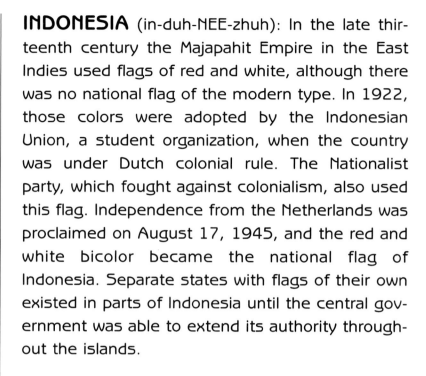

IRAN (i-RAN): The national colors—green for Islam, white for peace, and red for valor—were used in various Iranian flags during the nineteenth century. The modern tricolor was established in 1906 when Iran acquired its first constitution. In the center it included the Iranian coat of arms—a sun rising over a lion holding a sword. The revolution of 1979 introduced the Arabic inscription translated as "God Is Great" written twenty-two times along the stripe edges to recall the date the revolution began (22 Bahram in the Iranian calendar). The emblem in the center includes symbols of the globe, two crescents, and the word "Allah."

IRAQ (i-RAK): Several flags have been used by Iraq since it became independent in 1932, but all have included the pan-Arab colors (see *Kuwait*)— white, green, red, and black—based on an old Arab poem. The current flag of Iraq with three stars was adopted in 1963, when it was intended to symbolize a union of that country with Syria and Egypt that was never finalized. On January 14, 1991, the Arabic inscription that translates as "God Is Great," in the handwriting of President Saddam Hussein, was added between the stars to reflect the dedication of the people to the Islamic faith.

IRELAND (IRE-luhnd): For several centuries the traditional but unofficial national flag of Ireland was green with a central yellow harp. In the nineteenth century the colors of the two principal religious groups in Ireland, green for the Catholics and orange for the Protestants, were combined with white symbolizing peace. The new tricolor slowly became popular among national revolutionary groups, especially in 1848. It was not until 1917, however, that the tricolor was generally accepted as the national flag of Ireland.

ISRAEL (IZ-ree-uhl): In 1891 the basic design of the flag eventually adopted by Israel was first displayed at a Jewish temple in Brookline, Massachusetts; others later developed similar designs. That flag came to be used by the Zionist movement, which from 1897 onward struggled for Israeli independence. The colors blue and white had often been those of the *tallis*, or traditional Jewish prayer shawl, and the Shield of David has been used as a Jewish symbol for centuries. Following its proclamation of independence on May 14, 1948, Israel adopted the flag on November 12 of that year.

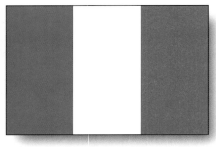

ITALY (IH-tehl-ee): The success of the French Revolution inspired many Italians. They rallied under a similar tricolor, chosen on February 25, 1797, by the new Cispadane Republic in northern Italy. Its colors of green, white, and red were based on military uniforms from Milan. Gradually, the many independent states that made up Italy, each with its own flag, united. On March 23, 1848, during a war with Austria, King Charles Albert of Sardinia recognized the tricolor for use in all his territories. Italy finally achieved complete unification in 1870 under this flag. The royal coat of arms featured on its central stripe was omitted in 1946 when Italy became a republic.

48

JAMAICA (juh-MAY-kuh): At the time of its adoption, the meaning of the national flag was summed up in the phrase "Hardships there are, but the land is green and the sun shineth." It was also stated that the green was for agriculture, the yellow for sunlight, and the black for the majority of the people. The flag was first officially hoisted on August 6, 1962, at the time the country gained its independence. The distinctive saltire (diagonal cross) was chosen to avoid duplicating the flag of Tanganyika, which had horizontal green, yellow, and black stripes like the original proposal for the Jamaican flag.

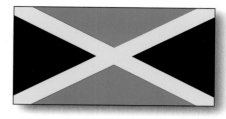

JAPAN (juh-PAN): Flags with a sun symbol have been used in Japan dating from at least the twelfth century. No national flag was introduced, however, until August 5, 1854, when the country began commercial contacts with other nations and needed an ensign for its ships. In 1870 the same Sun Disk Flag was approved for use on land. The red sun refers to the nickname for Japan—Land of the Rising Sun—and to the mythical origin of the first emperor as the son of the sun goddess Amaterasu. The national flag was confirmed on August 13, 1999.

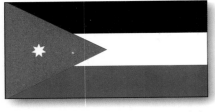

JORDAN (JOR-dehn): The first king of Transjordan (as the country was then called) was Abdullah, son of King Husayn ibn Ali of the Hijaz who created the Arab Revolt Flag in 1917 to resist the rule of the Ottoman Turks. It had horizontal stripes of black, green, and white, plus a red triangle at the hoist. The colors (see *Kuwait*) were taken from a thirteenth-century poem. Later, the position of the green and white stripes was changed, and a white star was added to the triangle of the flag as used in Transjordan. The flag was recognized on April 16, 1928, and the name of the country was changed to Jordan in 1946.

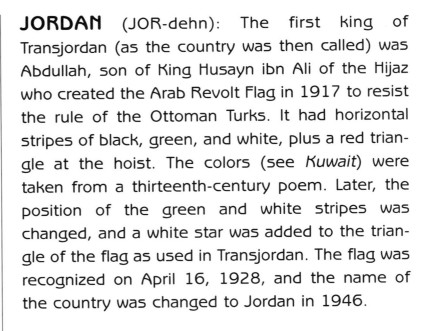

KAZAKHSTAN (kah-zak-STAN): Light blue has been the traditional color of the Turkic and Mongol peoples for many centuries: It refers to the sky under which these nomadic peoples travel. In the nineteenth century, however, at the time they came under Russian rule, the Kazakhs had no national flag. After it gained independence from the Soviet Union, Kazakhstan adopted its national flag in June 1992. The blue background is for peace and well-being. The eagle and sun stand for high ideals and freedom. A distinctive band of traditional Kazakh ornamentation is set at the hoist of the flag.

KENYA (KEH-nyuh): In 1951, the Kenya African Union, a political party, created a flag of black and red with an arrow and shield in the center. Later, the flag was modified to black-red-green stripes, and the organization became the Kenya African National Union (KANU). That KANU flag formed the basis for the national flag hoisted on December 12, 1963, when Kenya became independent. The struggle for freedom is symbolized by the red, agriculture by the green, and the majority local population by the black. The traditional weapons, including spears and a Masai shield, recall the people's struggle for independence.

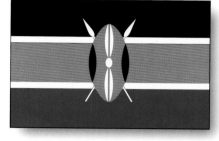

KIRIBATI (KIR-uh-bas): A coat of arms had been granted to the Gilbert Islands in 1937 by the British government, which administered that territory in the Pacific Ocean. On July 12, 1979, the Gilberts became independent, and the spelling of the national name was changed to Kiribati, the local pronunciation of the word *Gilberts*. The new flag, based on the coat of arms, showed the waters of the Pacific below a rising sun and the typical local frigate bird (a family of tropical seabirds). Kiribati is one of the few countries in the world whose flag and coat of arms are exactly the same.

KOREA, NORTH (kuh-REE-uh): The Russians occupied the northern part of Korea after World War II. The Communist government created in that territory proclaimed the Democratic People's Republic of Korea on September 9, 1948, under a flag that had been adopted on July 10. (Previously, North Korea used the same flag as South Korea.) The commitment of the country to communism was symbolized by the red star and the red stripe of the new flag. The white stripes were meant to stand for dignity, strength, and purity. The blue stripes stood for the nation's commitment to peace.

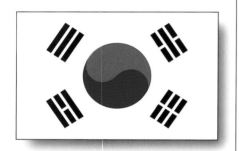

KOREA, SOUTH (kuh-REE-uh): The first national flag of Korea was adopted on August 18, 1882, utilizing ancient symbols of the nation. White stands for peace and the traditional clothing worn by Koreans. The central *t'aeguk*, or yin-yang, emblem is an old Chinese symbol representing such opposites as light and dark, good and evil, old and new, and male and female. The black bars, some broken and some unbroken, stand for the four seasons, the four cardinal directions, as well as the sun, moon, earth, and heaven. The flag was adopted by the Republic of Korea in 1950 and confirmed in October 1997.

KUWAIT (koo-WATE): On November 24, 1961, four months after Kuwait became independent, it adopted a national flag to replace the one then in use, a red banner bearing the country name in white Arabic script. The colors of the new design referred to the symbolism expressed in a thirteenth-century poem—green, for the lands of the Arabs; black, for the battles they fight to preserve those lands; red, for the blood on their swords; and white, for the purity of the warriors. The design of the flag is similar to those of other Arab nations, which have intentionally expressed both nationalism and pan-Arab unity in their flags.

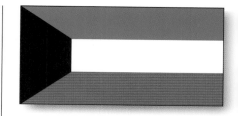

KYRGYZSTAN (kir-gih-STAN): The traditional home of the Kyrgyz people, the yurt, is constructed of wooden poles covered by heavy carpets. To allow smoke from cooking inside to escape, the yurt has an opening at the top. That opening forms the central emblem of the national flag adopted by Kyrgyzstan on March 3, 1992. It is shown on a yellow sun with forty rays, recalling the tribes of the Kyrgyz people united by their national hero, Manas the Noble. His flag is said to have been red; red flags were also used when Kyrgyzstan was under Soviet rule from 1924 to 1991.

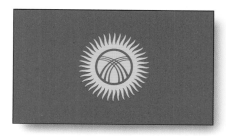

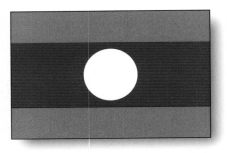

LAOS (LAH-ose): In 1950 the Pathet Lao (Communist forces in Laos) created a new symbol—a flag with stripes of red, blue, and red. The red stood for the blood of those fighting for national freedom and independence. The future prosperity of the country was symbolized by the blue. In the center of the flag was a white disk. The disk was borrowed from the national flag of Japan because it had promoted the independence of Asian countries from Western colonialism. In 1975 the Pathet Lao finally came to power, and their banner became the national flag of Laos on December 2.

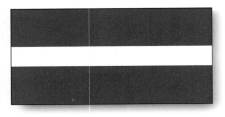

LATVIA (LAT-vee-uh): In 1870 students in Latvia, then a part of the Russian Empire, wanted a flag for their native land. Historian Janis Grinbergs discovered a book from 1279 describing a flag used by Latvians. That dark red banner with a narrow white horizontal stripe in the center became the modern symbol of Latvia. It was hoisted in 1918, when the country proclaimed its independence from Russia. It disappeared in 1940 when the Soviet Union annexed Latvia, but a half century later it was reestablished. Today the distinctive crimson (dark red) and white flag represents Latvia and all people of Latvian heritage.

LEBANON (LEH-buh-nuhn): In the Bible reference is made to the "cedars of Lebanon." These famous trees were a symbol of wealth and strength. When the Christian population of Lebanon formed a battalion to fight together with the French in World War I, a cedar tree appeared on their flag. In 1920, when the French established Lebanon as a territory, its flag was the tricolor of France with a cedar in the center. In 1943, following the independence of Lebanon, a new flag was created. The red and white stripes of the new design were associated with traditional clans living in Lebanon.

LESOTHO (luh-SOO-too): The mountainous kingdom of Lesotho was under the protection of the British for a century. Its first national flag was created at the time the country achieved its independence on October 4, 1966. It had three vertical stripes of green, red, and blue with a Sotho straw hat in white silhouette. That flag was replaced on January 20, 1987, after the army overthrew the government. The new flag has stripes of green for prosperity and blue for life-giving rain. In the upper hoist corner appear traditional Sotho weapons—a shield, assegai, and knobkerrie—and ostrich feathers. These symbolize the defense of national independence.

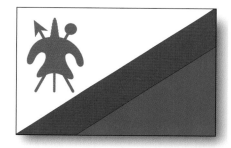

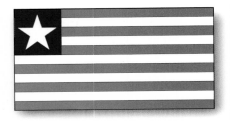

LIBERIA (lie-BUHR-ee-uh): In the early nineteenth century many Americans tried to help Africans who had been enslaved return to their home continent. The American Colonization Society purchased land in West Africa and named the area Liberia—land of the free. The flag of the society was the same as the Stars and Stripes except that a Christian cross replaced the stars. When Liberia proclaimed its independence on July 26, 1847, a new flag was needed. A star for independence replaced the cross, and the eleven signers of the Liberian Declaration of Independence were honored by the eleven stripes in the new flag.

LIBYA (LIH-bee-uh): The world's only monochromatic (one-color) national flag belongs to Libya. The green color stands for the nation's Green Revolution. Libya used to be a rich farming area, but deserts gradually took over most of the land. Today Libya is seeking to use water and modern technology to restore its former agricultural wealth. Green is also a favorite color in Islamic history, and Libya is a Muslim nation. The green flag, adopted in November 1977, replaced an earlier flag that had symbolized pan-Arab unity. The green flag is the fourth one that Libya has used since obtaining independence in 1951.

LIECHTENSTEIN (LEEK-tuhn-stine): The servants of Prince Joseph Wenzel of Liechtenstein wore uniforms of blue and red in the eighteenth century. These colors first appeared as a flag in the nineteenth century. The plain blue and red stripes represented Liechtenstein in the 1936 Olympic Games, where the same national flag was flown by Haiti. In 1937, therefore, Liechtenstein added a crown on the blue stripe to create a distinctive design. The crown symbolizes the link between Liechtenstein's prince and its people. Blue is for the sky, and red stands for the evening home fires in this tiny country.

LITHUANIA (lih-thuh-WAY-nee-uh): The traditional banner of Lithuania was red with a white knight on a horse. When Lithuania became independent in 1918, a special committee proposed a new design with horizontal stripes of yellow, green, and red. It first flew on November 11, 1918, and four years later, after Russia acknowledged Lithuanian independence, the tricolor was officially adopted. Red is for courage and love of country, green stands for the forests of Lithuania and for hope, and yellow symbolizes freedom and the rich fields of wheat. The flag was readopted in 1989, when Lithuania sought independence from the Soviet Union.

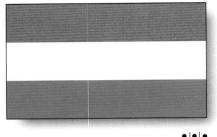

LUXEMBOURG (LUK-sem-berg): Like many European countries, Luxembourg bases its national flag on its coat of arms. Its shield has a red lion against a background of white and blue horizontal stripes. The red-white-blue flag was first used about 1815 and was given recognition by other countries when Luxembourg became independent in 1867. There is no symbolism associated with the colors. The arms dates from the early thirteenth century, at a time when the lion was an important symbol of royal dignity and power. The flag is similar to the one used by the Netherlands, but this is only a coincidence.

MACEDONIA (mah-suh-DOE-nee-uh): Red and black flags were used by the Slavic peoples of Macedonia in their revolution of 1903; their historic coat of arms showed a yellow lion on a crimson shield. Under Communist rule as part of Yugoslavia (1945–1991), the Republic of Macedonia used a yellow and red flag. In 1992 independent Macedonia chose a yellow star-burst symbol for its red flag. Greece claimed that this was a Greek rather than a Slavic symbol, and in 1995 Macedonia chose a new flag. The star burst was replaced by a golden sun, a symbol mentioned in the Macedonian national anthem.

MADAGASCAR (mah-duh-GAS-kuhr): In the past many of the kingdoms existing on the island of Madagascar used white and red flags. The most famous was the Merina, or Hova, kingdom. Its white and red flags disappeared when the island became a French colony in the late nineteenth century. A new national flag was adopted on October 21, 1958, when local self-government was established. The traditional red and white colors, standing for purity and sovereignty, were included in the new flag, still in use today. A stripe of green, standing for hope and the coastal regions of Madagascar, was also included in the design.

MALAWI (muh-LAH-wee): The name of the country means "flaming waters," which refers to Lake Malawi when the sun is setting. That idea suggested the sun symbol that appears on the national flag. The three stripes were originally used by the movement that struggled for independence, the Malawi Congress party. The color green refers to the lush green landscape of the country. Red is for the blood of those who died seeking independence. Black is a reminder of the African people who live in Malawi. The flag became official on July 6, 1964, when Malawi, formerly known as Nyasaland, achieved independence from Great Britain.

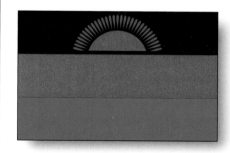

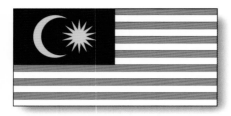

MALAYSIA (muh-LAY-zhuh): Red and white have long been popular among Malays. The flag of Malaya (as it was then called) was created in a 1950 competition. The red and white stripes referred to the eleven states, united in the 1946 Malayan Union. The blue canton of the flag indicated links to Great Britain and the Commonwealth. It bore a star and crescent for Islam in the royal color of Malaya, yellow. On September 16, 1963, the points on the star and the stripes of the flag, first hoisted on May 26, 1950, were increased to fourteen. These represented new states that joined the country, renamed Malaysia at that time.

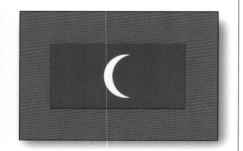

MALDIVES (MAHL-deevz): Many Arab countries in the Indian Ocean, including the Maldives, used a national flag of plain red. In the early twentieth century, increasing commerce required that ships have distinctive national flags, and the Maldives modified its red flag. A green rectangle with a white crescent was added to the center, and a black and white striped band appeared at the hoist. When the Maldives became independent on July 26, 1965, the black and white stripes were omitted from the flag. The crescent and color green stand for the Muslim faith of the Maldivian people; red is for the sacrifice of national heroes.

MALI (MAH-lee): Many West African countries feature the colors green, yellow, and red in their national flags. The African Democratic Rally, a political organization in the French colonies, originally chose those colors. They also appeared in the flag of Ethiopia, the oldest independent African nation. These colors came to be known as the pan-African colors because of their wide use on flags. In January 1959, Mali was united with Senegal under a common flag of green-yellow-red vertical stripes. In the center was a traditional Mali symbol—a black stylized human figure. In 1960, Mali and Senegal separated, and on March 1, 1961, Mali omitted the human figure from its flag. Since that time it has displayed the simple tricolor in the pan-African colors.

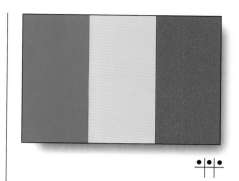

MALTA (MAWL-tuh): In the upper hoist corner of the Maltese national flag appears an image of the George Cross. This military decoration was granted by King George VI of Great Britain in 1942 to honor the resistance of Malta to the Nazis. From 1943 until the country became independent on September 21, 1964, the traditional white-red vertical bicolor of Malta showed the George Cross on a blue canton. Legend attributes the white and red stripes of the flag to Count Roger I in the eleventh century, although their use in Malta is documented only since the sixteenth century.

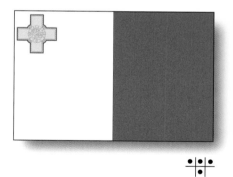

MARSHALL ISLANDS (MAHR-shul IE-lunds):
The Pacific Ocean is symbolized by the blue background of the national flag. The increasing width of the stripes on the flag suggests the growth and vitality of the nation. Orange is for wealth and bravery, while white symbolizes brightness. The unique star has twenty-four points, referring to the municipalities of the country. The four long star rays hint at the cross of Christianity, the faith of most Marshall Islanders. The national flag was introduced on May 1, 1979, together with local self-government. The flag was designed by Emlain Kabua, the wife of the first president.

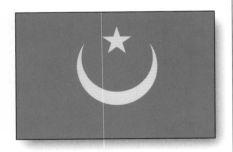

MAURITANIA (mawr-uh-TAY-nee-uh): Throughout
most of its history, Mauritania has been controlled by the Muslim people of the north rather than the black Africans of its southern regions. That dominance is reflected in the national flag adopted on April 1, 1959. The green background and the crescent and star are traditional Islamic symbols. No change was made in the flag when the country became independent on November 28, 1960. The crescent is a very ancient symbol favored by Muslims and others throughout Africa and Asia. The earliest known usage has been found in the ancient civilizations located in what is today Iraq.

MAURITIUS (maw-RIH-shee-us): When the island of Mauritius, then a British colony, became independent on March 12, 1968, a new national flag was hoisted; it has never been altered since. The blue stripe stands for the Indian Ocean, where Mauritius is located. The subtropical climate and agricultural riches of the country are reflected in the green stripe. The yellow of the flag refers to "the light of freedom" that was achieved with independence. Red hints at the nation's struggle for independence. Mauritius is the only country with a flag of four plain equal horizontal stripes.

MEXICO (MEK-sih-koe): An eagle holding a snake while standing on a nopal cactus growing from a rock surrounded by water is an ancient Aztec symbol. It represents their founding of Tenochtitlán (now Mexico City) in 1325. After three centuries of Spanish rule Mexico became independent in 1821. The stripes of its tricolor, adopted at that time, were symbolic: green for independence, white for the Roman Catholic religion, and red for union. Mexico subsequently was a kingdom, an empire, and then a republic. Each regime had a slightly different version of the coat of arms in the center of the national tricolor.

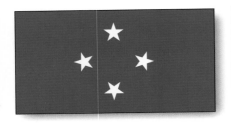

MICRONESIA (mie-kruh-NEE-zhuh): Following World War II, Pacific islands that had been ruled by Japan came under American administration, supervised by the United Nations. They formed the Trust Territory of the Pacific Islands (TTPI); its territorial flag was adopted on United Nations Day (October 24) in 1962. The flag was blue with six white stars for the districts, and the colors referred to the United Nations flag. When Micronesia separated from the TTPI, it adopted a similar flag with only four stars, representing its own subdivisions. Following Micronesian independence on November 3, 1986, a darker blue was substituted for the original UN blue.

MOLDOVA (mahl-DOE-vuh): Blue, yellow, and red have been Romanian national colors since the nineteenth century. Moldova shares the language and culture of Romania and at times has been part of that country. Under Communist rule the flags of Moldova were red or red and green. Just before achieving independence in 1991, Moldova adopted the Romanian tricolor as its national flag. In the center was its new coat of arms featuring an eagle with sword, cross, and olive branch, the head of an ox, a crescent, a star, and a flower. Each of these symbols has a long history in the nation's civic heraldry.

MONACO (MAH-nuh-koe): The coat of arms of this tiny principality on the southern coast of France dates from the early fourteenth century. Its shield consists of red and white diamonds, which gave Monaco its national colors. Over the centuries Monaco has used different flags—most frequently a version of the princely coat of arms on a white field. On April 4, 1881, however, that flag was limited for use only on government buildings and by the ruling prince. The national flag became a simple horizontal bicolor of red over white. There is no symbolism officially associated with these colors.

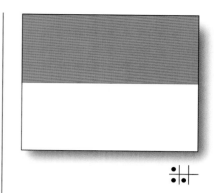

MONGOLIA (mahn-GOLE-ee-yuh): The national flag of Mongolia was red with gold symbols when China recognized the independence of the country in 1945. It also included a stripe of light blue in the center because historically that color represented the Mongolian people. The symbols on the flag have both ancient and modern meanings. Originally the design, known as the soyonbo, expressed Buddhist religious values. The star of communism appeared over the soyonbo until the one-party government ended in 1992. Possible new designs were considered for the Mongolian flag, but on January 12, 1992, it was decided to retain the 1945 flag except for the Communist star.

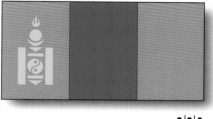

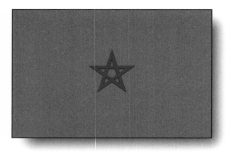

MOROCCO (muh-RAH-koe): Different Muslim dynasties controlled Morocco from the early Middle Ages onward. Each dynasty utilized military flags of a single color on which religious inscriptions were written. A plain red flag frequently was used by ships to represent Morocco in the nineteenth century, and similar flags were flown by other Muslim states of North Africa. In the early twentieth century the country became a French protectorate. To make its red flag distinctive, a green emblem called a "Seal of Solomon" was added to it on November 17, 1915. That ancient symbol is found on buildings, manuscripts, clothing, and in other forms in Morocco.

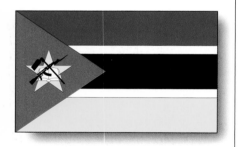

MOZAMBIQUE (moe-zuhm-BEEK): A 1974 agreement for the transition to independence of Mozambique, long a Portuguese colony, was signed by Portugal and the Liberation Front of Mozambique (FRELIMO). Their flags flew jointly from September 5, 1974, until June 25, 1975. After gaining freedom, Mozambique chose an entirely new flag. The current national flag of Mozambique, hoisted in April 1983, is based on that of FRELIMO with a special symbol added to the red triangle. The hoe stands for peasants, the book for education, and the rifle for national defense.

MYANMAR (MYAHN-mahr): During World War II the Anti-Fascist Organization (AFO) fought against Japanese occupation of the country, then known as Burma. The AFO flag was red with a white star in the upper hoist corner. After the war, the Burmese opposed the reestablishment of the British colonial regime. Independence was finally achieved on January 4, 1948, and the flag of the Anti-Fascist Organization was modified. The new national flag had a large white star and five small white stars on a blue canton, the rest of the flag being red. On January 4, 1974, the five stars were replaced by a cogwheel and ears of rice, standing for industry and agriculture.

NAMIBIA (nuh-MIH-bee-uh): In anticipation of its national independence on March 21, 1990, Namibia had a flag-designing contest in which almost a thousand proposals were submitted. The pattern finally adopted on February 2 incorporated the blue-red-green colors found in the flag of the South West Africa People's Organization, which had struggled for national independence. In the national flag, blue refers to the Atlantic Ocean on which the country borders and for the sky. Green is for agriculture, red recalls the commitment to a better future, and white is for unity and peace. The golden sun symbolizes life and energy.

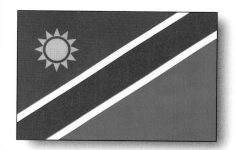

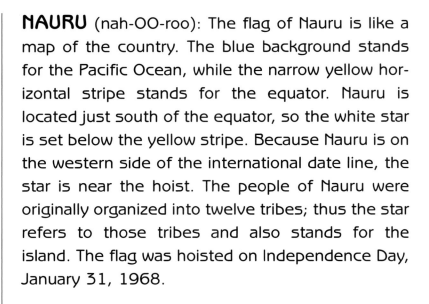

NAURU (nah-OO-roo): The flag of Nauru is like a map of the country. The blue background stands for the Pacific Ocean, while the narrow yellow horizontal stripe stands for the equator. Nauru is located just south of the equator, so the white star is set below the yellow stripe. Because Nauru is on the western side of the international date line, the star is near the hoist. The people of Nauru were originally organized into twelve tribes; thus the star refers to those tribes and also stands for the island. The flag was hoisted on Independence Day, January 31, 1968.

NEPAL (nuh-PAWL): The Hindu kingdom of Nepal in the Himalayas is the only modern country that does not have a rectangular national flag. Two united triangles were common in traditional flags of the Indian subcontinent in the past. The sun and moon are also ancient symbols, frequently found in the decoration and art of Nepal. They suggest that the country will live as long as the sun and moon exist. The current form of the flag, adopted as part of the new national constitution on December 16, 1962, omits the facial features that used to appear on the sun and moon.

NETHERLANDS (NEH-thur-lendz): This simple tricolor was one of the first true national flags, and it may have inspired the French tricolor. Dutch soldiers in the Eighty Years' War (1568–1648) used the orange-white-blue colors of their leader, Prince William of Orange, for their military banners and ship ensigns. Similar colors were found in many of the coats of arms of the provinces that made up the United Netherlands. Over time, the orange of the flag was replaced by red. The first law establishing the red-white-blue Dutch flag dates from 1796, although the flag itself had already been in use for two hundred years.

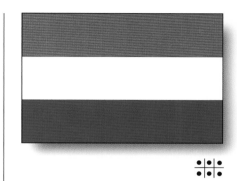

NEW ZEALAND (noo ZEE-luhnd): For centuries the Southern Cross constellation has been considered a distinctive symbol in the Southern Hemisphere. New Zealand first employed the Southern Cross in its flag of 1869 on a background of blue. The British Union Jack appeared in the canton; like other colonies, New Zealand inserted its badge at the fly end of the flag. That design is basically the same one in use today—four white-bordered red stars. The Union Jack indicates traditional links with Great Britain. This design became the official national flag of New Zealand on June 12, 1902.

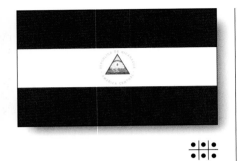

NICARAGUA (nih-kuh-RAH-gwuh): Following independence in 1823, Central America adopted a flag of horizontal blue-white-blue stripes. A number of national flags were used by Nicaragua after it broke from that union. In 1908, however, the old flag of blue-white-blue stripes was readopted with the Nicaraguan coat of arms added in the center. The exact flag design in use today dates from August 27, 1971. The five volcanoes in the central emblem stand for Nicaragua and the other four Central American nations with which it was originally united. The design also includes a red liberty cap on a pole and a triangle symbolizing equality.

NIGER (nee-ZHAIR): The territory of this West African country includes fertile lands along the Niger River and desert regions in the north and east. The former areas are symbolized by the green stripe in the national flag. The orange stripe recalls the deserts, while the central orange sun hints at the tropical location of the country. Purity, innocence, and civic duty are symbolized by the white stripe of the flag. Niger was a French colony before achieving independence on August 3, 1960. The flag was adopted on November 23, 1959; the French tricolor alone flew over Niger prior to that date.

NIGERIA (nie-JEER-ee-uh): A Nigerian student, Michael Taiwo Akinkunmi, saw the vast fields and forests of his native land while flying to school in London. When he entered the flag-designing contest that Nigeria held in 1958, his design therefore included two green stripes. The white band between them was for unity and peace. (He also had placed a red sun on the white stripe, which the competition judges decided to omit.) Akinkunmi's winning design became the national flag of Nigeria on its national Independence Day, October 1, 1960. Three thousand other designs had been submitted for consideration.

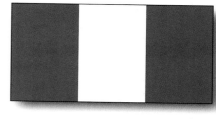

NORWAY (NAWR-way): For centuries Norway was ruled by Denmark, whose national flag was red with a white cross. In 1821, when Norway was under Swedish rule, the Norwegian parliament adopted its own national flag. It was red with a white cross, but had a blue cross superimposed over the white. The kings of Sweden insisted that Swedish symbols be included in the flag when it flew on ships. Norwegians fought to have the right to a "clean flag" and were finally successful in 1899. The flag of 1821, designed by Frederik Meltzer, has been used by Norway since then, both on land and at sea.

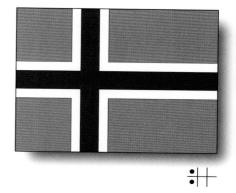

71

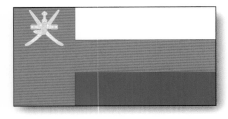

OMAN (o-MAHN): The three colors of the national flag of Oman have historical symbolism. The sultans who ruled the country long displayed a red flag, while the imam (religious leader) flew a flag of white. The country's interior has an area known as Green Mountain. Today, the green in the flag officially stands for the fertility of the land. Red is for the struggle against foreign invaders, and white stands for prosperity and peace. The present design, dating from November 18, 1995, includes typical Omani crossed swords, dagger, and belt. The basic flag was chosen on December 17, 1970.

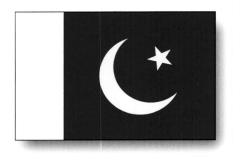

PAKISTAN (PA-kih-stan): For centuries the British ruled most of the Indian subcontinent under the Union Jack. When the All-India Muslim League was founded in December 1906, their goal was independence for a new country—Pakistan—to include those parts of India populated by Muslims. The Muslim League flag adopted at that time was green with a white star and crescent, both Islamic symbols. When Pakistan achieved its independence on August 14, 1947, the flag of the Muslim League was modified to form the new national banner. A white vertical stripe was added at the hoist to stand for minority religious groups.

PALAU (puh-LAU): A local government was established for Palau on January 1, 1981. It had previously been part of the Trust Territory of the Pacific Islands, governed by the United States under United Nations supervision. A new flag was hoisted at that time, chosen from more than a thousand proposals. The background of the flag was blue to symbolize the transition to self-government. (Many other national flags of the Pacific Ocean area are also blue.) Near the hoist was a yellow full moon standing for peace, tranquillity, love, and domestic unity. The flag continued in use after Palau became independent in October 1994.

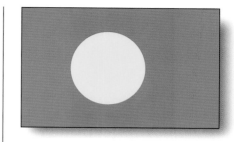

PANAMA (PA-nuh-mah): For many years Panamanians were unhappy with their status as part of Colombia. When the Colombians rejected a treaty with the United States concerning the building of a Panama Canal, a revolt in Panama quickly led to independence. The flag for the new country was adopted on July 4, 1904. The colors red and blue were said to symbolize the local political parties (Liberals and Conservatives); white was for peace between them. The flag was designed by Manuel E. Amador, son of the first Panamanian president. Many ships are registered in Panama, making its flag well known in the ports of the world.

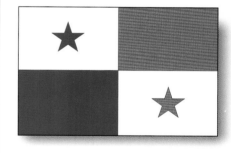

PAPUA NEW GUINEA (PA-poo-wuh noo GIH-nee): The Australians, who governed both Papua and New Guinea, proposed a flag to be used when those territories united. During an introductory tour by officials to present that flag, a young student submitted an entirely different design. Susan Karike suggested using red and black because these were colors widely found in local clothing and art. Her design also included the Southern Cross constellation and a bird of paradise in yellow silhouette. The design was officially recognized in 1971, and four years later it became the national flag for all purposes when Papua New Guinea achieved independence on September 16, 1975.

PARAGUAY (PAR-uh-gwie): The flag of Paraguay is unique because it is the only national banner with a different design on either side. The obverse (front) bears the national coat of arms, which has the star of independence and the name of the country in Spanish. On the reverse of the flag, the seal of the national treasury is featured. It includes a lion, liberty cap, and the national motto "Peace and Justice." The red-white-blue colors of the flag were chosen by President José Rodríguez de Francia, based on the tricolor of France. The Paraguayan flag has been used since at least 1842.

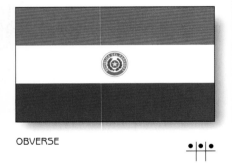

OBVERSE

REVERSE

74

PERU (puh-ROO): In the eighteenth century, Peru was under the rule of Spain, which had a national flag of horizontal red-yellow-red stripes bearing a coat of arms. The national flag of Peru, adopted in March 1822, had horizontal stripes of red-white-red with the Peruvian coat of arms. To make the flag more distinctive, the stripes were changed to a vertical position in May 1822. Finally, the current coat of arms and flag were adopted on February 25, 1825. The red stands for the blood of patriots, while the white stripe is for purity. The coat of arms bears a vicuña (an animal related to the llama), cinchona tree, and cornucopia.

PHILIPPINES (fih-luh-PEENZ): The struggle for independence from Spain began in the Philippines in 1898 under a flag similar to the present one. The Masonic triangle is a symbol of liberty. Its eight-rayed gold sun and three gold stars stand for the eight provinces where the Philippine revolution began and the three main islands in the country—Luzon, Visayan, and Mindanao. The stripes are red for courage and blue for sacrifice. Independence was finally achieved on July 4, 1946, under the same basic flag, although the shade of blue was changed on September 16, 1997. The flag is flown with its red stripe on top during wartime.

75

POLAND (POE-luhnd): The coat of arms of Poland consists of a red shield with a crowned white eagle, a design that has been used since the thirteenth century. The eagle was probably chosen as a symbol because it represented royal power. The national flag of Poland, adopted in 1919, uses the colors of the shield to form a horizontal bicolor. Polish symbols were forbidden under the Nazi occupation of Poland from 1939 until 1945. Under the Communist regime that existed from 1945 until 1990, the golden crown on the head of the eagle in the coat of arms was removed.

PORTUGAL (PAWR-chih-gul): The coat of arms of Portugal, appearing on its flag, dates from the twelfth century. The original white shield bore five small blue shields forming a cross, symbolizing the Portuguese struggle against the ruling Muslim dynasty. A century later a red border with gold castles was added; the castles referred to a new territory, the Algarve. Behind the shield is a navigational instrument known as an armillary sphere, a reminder of the many explorations undertaken by Portuguese navigators. The green and red colors of the flag were adopted on June 30, 1911, a year after Portugal's monarchy was overthrown.

QATAR (KAH-tuhr): The maroon and white national flag design, which may date from the nineteenth century, is similar to the flag of nearby Bahrain. Similar flags of red or red and white have been hoisted for centuries by Arab merchants sailing in the Arabian Gulf and on local forts. Originally, the flag of Qatar was decorated with crimson diamonds between the serrations (zigzag pattern) or with the name of the country in Arabic script. Independence from Britain was achieved by Qatar on September 3, 1971, but no change was made in the flag.

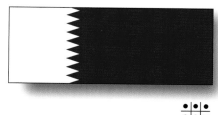

ROMANIA (ruh-MAY-nee-uh): A revolution in 1848 introduced the vertical blue-yellow-red national flag of Romania. Its colors were based on old symbols used by Romanian territories, especially Walachia and Moldavia. After the defeat of the revolutionaries the flag was not forgotten. In 1861 a horizontal form of the tricolor was adopted and finally, six years later, the vertical tricolor was reestablished. Kings and Communists later introduced special coats of arms on the yellow stripe to symbolize their governments. On December 27, 1989, after the fall of communism, it was decided to recognize the plain tricolor as the Romanian national flag.

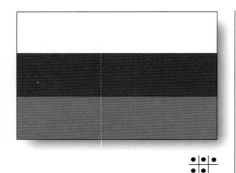

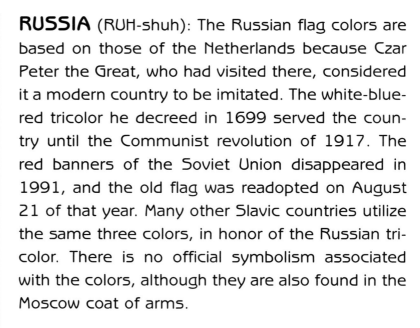

RUSSIA (RUH-shuh): The Russian flag colors are based on those of the Netherlands because Czar Peter the Great, who had visited there, considered it a modern country to be imitated. The white-blue-red tricolor he decreed in 1699 served the country until the Communist revolution of 1917. The red banners of the Soviet Union disappeared in 1991, and the old flag was readopted on August 21 of that year. Many other Slavic countries utilize the same three colors, in honor of the Russian tricolor. There is no official symbolism associated with the colors, although they are also found in the Moscow coat of arms.

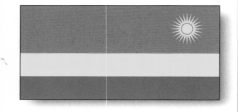

RWANDA (roo-AHN-dah): On July 1, 1962, Rwanda became an independent country. Its first national flag had three equal vertical stripes of red, yellow, and green (see *Mali*). The center of that flag had a black R to stand for the name of the country, as well as revolution and referendum. After hundreds of thousands of Rwandans died in the genocide wars of 1994, it was felt that the country should have a new flag that symbolized peace. The current national flag was therefore adopted on December 31, 2001. The blue stripe stands for peace and happiness, and its golden sun represents unity and the struggle against ignorance. The center stripe is for economic development while the bottom stripe symbolizes prosperity.

ST. KITTS AND NEVIS (saint kits and NEE-vus): The black stripe of this flag recalls the African origin of most of the local population. The golden sun is suggested by the yellow stripe borders. Green and red stand respectively for agriculture and the fight for independence. The two stars are for the islands and also are symbols of liberty and hope. The flag was first hoisted on September 18, 1983, when St. Kitts-Nevis obtained its independence from Great Britain. The flag, chosen in a competition, was created by Edrice Lewis. It replaced an earlier flag used when the islands obtained self-government in 1967.

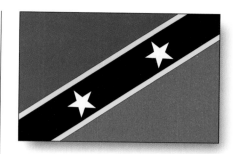

ST. LUCIA (saint LOO-shuh): Two extinct volcanic mountains on the island, known as the Pitons, are symbolized on the national flag by the black triangle. Tropical sunshine is reflected in the yellow triangle, while the blue background of the flag hints at the Atlantic Ocean and Caribbean Sea, between which St. Lucia is located. Harmony between different races is represented by the black and white colors of the flag. First hoisted on March 1, 1967, the flag was modified slightly at the time of the country's independence on February 22, 1979. It was designed by Dunstan St. Omar, a local artist.

ST. VINCENT AND THE GRENADINES (saint
VIN-sent and the greh-nuh-DEENZ): The three stripes on the national flag refer to lush vegetation and the vitality of the people (green), the island's beautiful beaches (yellow), and the sky and sea (blue). In the center are three diamonds that form a V, suggesting the name of the country. The flag had originally been adopted in 1979, but its central coat of arms was replaced by the three "gems" when a new government came into office. The new flag was first flown officially on October 22, 1985. Elaine Liverpool and Julien van der Wal both contributed to the design.

SAMOA (suh-MOE-uh): Courage (red), freedom
(blue), and purity (white) were chosen for the flag of Samoa because they were found in the flags of Great Britain and New Zealand, which administered the territory until its independence on January 1, 1962. The Southern Cross constellation in the canton is found in other flags of the Southern Hemisphere, including those of Australia, New Zealand, and Brazil. From 1948 until February 24, 1949, the flag of what was then called Western Samoa showed only four stars in the constellation.

SAN MARINO (san muh-REE-noe): This ancient country first used its national blue and white colors at the time of the French Revolution. The white stands for the clouds around the mountain where San Marino is located; blue is for the sky. The coat of arms on the flag was modified in 1862, when a crown was added at the top as a symbol of sovereignty. The three towers of San Marino City, each bearing an ostrich feather, are shown on the coat of arms. The national motto is Libertas, the Latin word for liberty, because San Marino is famous for welcoming refugees seeking freedom.

SÃO TOMÉ AND PRÍNCIPE (sow tuh-MAY and PRINT-sih-pay): The Movement for the Liberation of São Tomé and Príncipe (MLSTP) worked against Portuguese colonialism. When the country finally became independent on July 12, 1975, the new national flag chosen was basically the same as that used by the MLSTP. The tropical sun is reflected in the yellow stripe, while typical vegetation is symbolized by the green stripes. The stars featured on the flag correspond to the two islands that constitute the country and are featured in its name. The red triangle stands for the independence movement and for equality. These are considered the pan-African colors (see *Mali*).

SAUDI ARABIA (SOW-dee uh-RAY-bee-uh): Traditional Muslim flags have usually been of a solid color, often richly decorated with religious inscriptions. Green is the color traditionally associated with Fatima, the daughter of the Prophet Muhammad. The flag of Saudi Arabia, created in 1932, bears the testimony of Islam—"There is no God but Allah and Muhammad is the Prophet of Allah." The sword shows that the people of the country are militant in their religious beliefs. The Saudi flag is never supposed to be flown at half-staff or upside down because of the sacred symbolism of its design. Its current version dates from March 15, 1973.

SENEGAL (seh-nih-GAHL): The country became independent in September 1960, after having briefly been united with Mali. The flag of the Mali Federation at that time was a vertical tricolor of green-yellow-red with the stylized figure of a black man in the center. Senegal replaced that symbol with a green star. The colors are meant to stand for hope and Islam (green), natural riches (yellow), and socialism and life (red). These three colors are known as the pan-African colors (see *Mali*).

SEYCHELLES (say-SHEL): On June 29, 1976, Seychelles became independent. A year later an opposition political party overthrew the government and changed the national flag. The new flag was based on the flag of the party, which dominated the country. In 1993 it became necessary for the government to recognize other political parties. Parliament therefore decided to change the national flag so that it would not reflect the dominance of the former ruling group. The unique new flag incorporates colors for the land (green), justice and harmony (white), the people and their work (red), the sun (yellow), and the sea and sky (blue).

SIERRA LEONE (see-ER-uh lee-OWN): On April 27, 1961, the British colony of Sierra Leone became an independent nation. Its new national flag had three equal horizontal stripes of green, white, and blue. Those colors stand for the country's mountains and agriculture, for justice and unity, and for the wish to contribute to world peace. The blue also refers to the capital city, Freetown, which has an important natural harbor. The coat of arms of Sierra Leone includes the three colors, as well as a lion, because the name of the country means "Lion Mountain" in Portuguese. Explorers from Portugal were the first Europeans to visit the area.

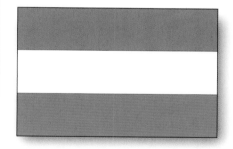

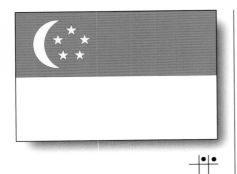

SINGAPORE (SING-uh-pawr): Many flags in Southeast Asia include the colors red and white. In the flag of Singapore they stand for equality and universal brotherhood and for virtue and purity. The flag became official on December 3, 1959, when Singapore obtained self-government. The five stars in the flag stand for equality, justice, progress, peace, and democracy. Unlike crescents in many national flags, the Singapore flag crescent does not represent Islam; instead it is the symbol of a growing young country. No change was made in the flag of Singapore when it became independent on August 9, 1965.

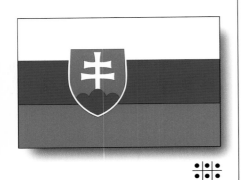

SLOVAKIA (sloe-VAH-kee-uh): In 1848 the Slavic people of what was then called Upper Hungary chose the well-known Slavic colors of white, blue, and red for their flag. They also modified the traditional Hungarian coat of arms—a red shield with a white cross rising from three green hills—by altering the green to blue. Those symbols, created in the nineteenth century, achieved official recognition in 1992. In anticipation of its independence on the first day of the next year, Slovakia adopted the white-blue-red tricolor—adding its national shield to distinguish it from the Russian flag.

SLOVENIA (sloe-VEE-nee-uh): The traditional shield of Slovenia was white with a blue eagle, bearing on its breast a red and white checkered crescent. White, blue, and red have also been the traditional Slavic colors since the Russian flag was created in 1699. Slovenians used the same tri-color flag from the early years of the nineteenth century, although it was part of Austria-Hungary and, later, of Yugoslavia. Slovenia finally obtained its independence on June 25, 1991. The new flag hoisted was white-blue-red with a coat of arms featuring its famous Triglav Mountain and yellow stars on blue for its Celje region.

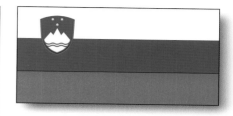

SOLOMON ISLANDS (SAH-luh-mun IE-lunds): The five original districts of the Solomon Islands were represented by the five stars on its new national flag, hoisted on November 18, 1977. The green triangle of the flag recalls the fertile land of the islands, while the blue hints at the importance of water (rivers and rain) and of the Pacific Ocean, where the Solomons are located. A yellow stripe representing the sun separates the triangles. The flag was created after long debates in parliament; no change was made when the Solomon Islands became independent on July 7, 1978.

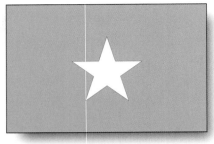

SOMALIA (soe-MAH-lee-uh): After World War II the former Italian colony of Somalia was put under United Nations supervision. In anticipation of independence, a national flag was created. It included the same colors (light blue and white) found in the United Nations flag. The five points on the central white star stand for five regions inhabited by Somali people. The flag was introduced on October 12, 1954, although Somalia did not become independent until July 1, 1960. Four days earlier the former British Somaliland became independent under the same flag before uniting with Somalia on July 1.

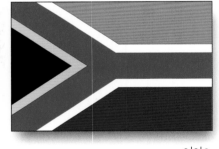

SOUTH AFRICA (sowth AH-frih-kuh): A peaceful revolutionary change took place in South Africa on April 27, 1994: Free universal elections terminated the apartheid regime and introduced a multiracial democratic government. This was symbolized by the new national flag raised on that date, designed by state herald Frederick Brownell. Individually, the six colors of the flag were traditional in South African flags; they have not been given any specific new symbolism. The pall, or Y-shape, stands for the coming together of many parts and the merging of past and present. Unique in design, the official new national flag quickly became very popular in South Africa.

SPAIN (spane): In 1785 the king decided to change the naval flag of Spain, previously white with the Spanish coat of arms in the center. Many traditional coats of arms in Spanish regions included the colors yellow and red. His choice for the new flag, therefore, was unequal horizontal stripes of red-yellow-red with the royal coat of arms. Many variations in the shield have occurred in the subsequent two centuries, but the basic design is still in use. Under the royal crown, the shield now contains emblems of Castile, León, Aragón, Navarre, and Granada. The traditional "pillars of Hercules" flank the shield.

SRI LANKA (sree LAHN-kuh): For many centuries the dominant Singhalese people of Sri Lanka used a red flag with a central golden lion for their country. After a century and a half of British rule, the island became independent in 1948 under the "Lion Flag." Minorities protested, however, that they were not represented in the national flag. Therefore, in March 1951, stripes of orange for the Tamils (Hindus) and green for the Muslims were added to the flag. The present design of the flag dates from September 7, 1978, when the bo leaves (a Buddhist symbol) in the corners of the crimson rectangle were modified.

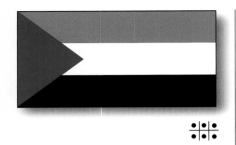

SUDAN (soo-DAN): Nationalists gained control of the Sudan in 1969. On May 20, 1970, they changed the national flag to the current design, based on the Arab Liberation Flag. It incorporates the colors green (standing for Islam and prosperity), red (for socialism, progress, and independence), and black (referring to the Arabic word *sudan*, which means black). The white of the flag refers to the revolutionary flag of 1924, as well as to optimism and peace. The same colors, often referred to as the pan-Arab colors (see *Kuwait*), had previously been used for flags in the Sudan in the nineteenth century, when nationalists expelled foreign troops.

SURINAME (SUHR-uh-nahm): After centuries of rule by the Netherlands, Suriname (also known as Dutch Guiana) became an independent nation on November 25, 1975. Its new national flag had been approved by parliament a few days before. Combining winning designs from a flag competition, legislators chose five horizontal stripes of green, white, and red. They stand respectively for the fields and jungles of the land, freedom and justice, and the progressive spirit of a young nation. The yellow star in the center suggests both unity and the golden future of Suriname, based on the sacrifices of its citizens.

SWAZILAND (SWAH-zee-land): During World War II a regiment of Swazi soldiers fighting with the Allies carried a battle flag very similar to the design now used as the national flag of Swaziland. Crimson is for the battles fought by the Swazis in the past, while blue is for peace. Yellow suggests the mineral wealth of the country. In the center is a traditional Swazi shield with two spears and a "fighting stick" bearing distinctive feathers. The flag of Swaziland was made official on October 30, 1967, and independence was achieved the following year on September 6.

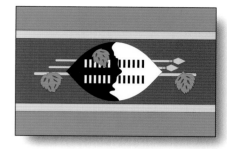

SWEDEN (SWEE-dehn): Centuries ago Sweden fought many battles with Denmark, whose flag had a white cross on a red background. The Swedish flag was based on the Danish banner: It was similar in design but with completely different colors. The blue and yellow probably came from one of two Swedish royal coats of arms. The design of the national flag dates from at least the sixteenth century, although the coats of arms are two hundred years older. The present form of the flag was established on June 22, 1906, the year after Norway separated from Sweden and ended use of the flag they had shared.

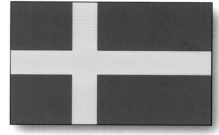

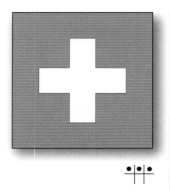

SWITZERLAND (SWIT-suhr-lund): The Imperial War Flag of the Holy Roman Empire was red, often with a white cross added to show that the army was serving a sacred cause. A flag of that design was used as early as 1240 by Schwyz, one of the three original cantons (states) of Switzerland. The modern Swiss national flag was created in 1889, although it had been used by the army for four decades. The national flag is square, but in 1941 the same white cross on red, with different proportions, was approved as an ensign for use by Swiss-registered vessels.

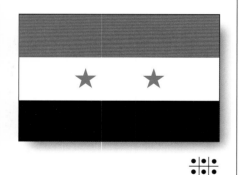

SYRIA (SUHR-ee-uh): Many flags were flown in the twentieth century by Syria, most of them incorporating the pan-Arab colors (see *Kuwait*) of green, white, black, and red. These colors had originally been used in the Arab Revolt Flag created in 1917 by King Husayn ibn Ali of the Hijaz, the father of Jordan's first king. When Syria joined with Egypt in 1958 to form the United Arab Republic, its flag had red-white-black stripes with two green stars. In 1961 the union ended, but Syria readopted the United Arab Republic flag as its own on March 29, 1980. The flag symbolizes the dedication of Syria to Arab unification.

TAIWAN (TIE-wahn): The Kuomintang (Nationalist party), a revolutionary organization, adopted its blue flag with a white twelve-rayed sun in 1895. In 1928 that flag was used as the canton for the new national flag of the Republic of China; the field was red. The three colors stand for the "Principles of the People"—nationalism, democracy, and socialism. After their defeat in a long Chinese civil war, Kuomintang forces retreated to the island of Taiwan in 1949. Their flag still flies today over that island—officially known as the Republic of China—although few countries recognize its government.

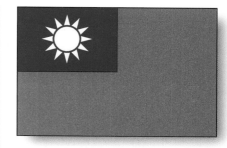

TAJIKISTAN (tah-jih-kih-STAN): Under Soviet rule, Tajikistan used a red flag with narrow horizontal stripes of white and green; it included the usual gold hammer, sickle, and star of communism. On September 9, 1991, Tajikistan became an independent country. The following year it chose a new national flag with the same colors as the old one. The red, white, and green stand for the sovereignty of the state, cotton as its principal crop, and other agricultural produce. The central golden design represents unity among the different classes of people living in Tajikistan. The new flag dates from November 24, 1992.

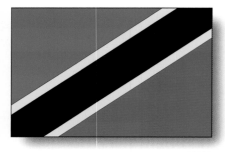

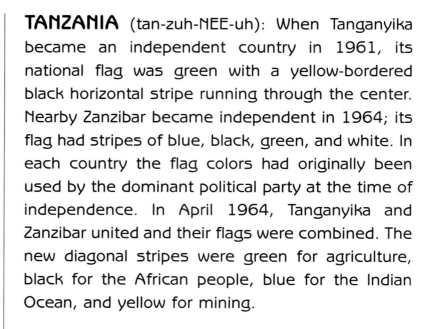

TANZANIA (tan-zuh-NEE-uh): When Tanganyika became an independent country in 1961, its national flag was green with a yellow-bordered black horizontal stripe running through the center. Nearby Zanzibar became independent in 1964; its flag had stripes of blue, black, green, and white. In each country the flag colors had originally been used by the dominant political party at the time of independence. In April 1964, Tanganyika and Zanzibar united and their flags were combined. The new diagonal stripes were green for agriculture, black for the African people, blue for the Indian Ocean, and yellow for mining.

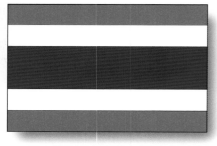

THAILAND (TIE-land): The original Thai national flag was plain red; then for decades the flag was red with a white elephant in the center. At the time of World War I the king decided to alter the flag. At first he chose five horizontal stripes of red and white, but on September 28, 1917, the central stripe was changed to blue. This was considered the color of the king, but it also gave Thailand the same three colors as its wartime allies—the "Colors of Liberty" used by the United States, Great Britain, France, and others. The elephant, still a favorite Thai symbol, appears on the war ensign.

TOGO (TOE-goe): The administrative regions of the country are symbolized by the five stripes of green and yellow in the national flag. The green recalls that most people in Togo rely on the land for their livelihood. Yellow suggests labor, while white symbolizes purity. The flag of Togo was adopted when the country became independent on April 27, 1960. Although it incorporates the pan-African colors of red, yellow, and green (see *Mali*), the design is unique to Togo. As a trust territory governed by France before 1960, Togo used a green flag with two yellow stars and the tricolor.

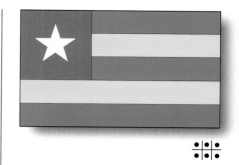

TONGA (TOHN-guh): Western missionaries converted people in Tonga to Christianity in the nineteenth century, and therefore a cross was chosen for the national symbol in the first Tongan flag. In 1866 a new design was introduced by King George Tupou I: Most of the flag was red but the canton was white with a red cross. That color referred to the blood shed at the Crucifixion of Jesus. The flag was confirmed when the new national constitution went into effect on November 4, 1875. According to Tongan law, the national flag design may never be changed.

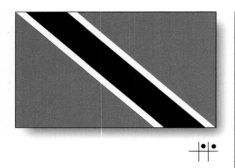

TRINIDAD AND TOBAGO (TRIH-nuh-dad and tuh-BAY-goe): The black of the national flag refers to the earth and the past, while white is for water and the present. The red suggests fire and the future of the nation, but is also explained as relating to the energy and vitality of the people. White symbolizes the unity between Trinidad and the smaller island of Tobago, and black stands for the people's dedication to strength in unity. The flag of Trinidad and Tobago was adopted on June 28, 1962, and was first officially hoisted at the time of independence on August 31 of the same year.

TUNISIA (too-NEE-zhuh): Many of the Muslim states along the coast of the southern Mediterranean for centuries flew a plain red naval flag, based on the Turkish ensigns formerly used there. In 1831 the bey, Tunisia's ruler, decided to add a distinctive symbol to the flag. He chose a white disk with a central red crescent and star. These traditional symbols had previously been featured in Tunisian jewelry, art, and architecture. Although France maintained a protectorate over Tunisia from 1881 to 1956, the national flag was not changed. In 1999 the star and crescent were modified.

TURKEY (TUR-kee): The Turkic people, who lived in Central Asia for many centuries before migrating to the area today known as Turkey, recognized red as their national color. The crescent and star was long used in the city of Constantinople (modern Istanbul) as a symbol of the victory of the Virgin Mary over the pagan goddess Diana, although it was also popular among Muslims. The current national flag of Turkey first began to be used in the late eighteenth century, the star having eight points at that time instead of five. After Turkey became a secular republic in 1923, no change was made in the flag.

TURKMENISTAN (turk-MEH-nuh-stan): On October 27, 1991, Turkmenistan, formerly a part of the Soviet Union since 1924, became independent. Its national flag was adopted the following February. It includes five intricate designs representing traditional carpet patterns that have been used by the Turkmen people for many centuries. The green flag background is a symbol of Islam, while the crescent stands for a bright future. The five stars of the flag refer to the five human senses. On February 19, 1997, a golden wreath resembling the one on the United Nations flag was added below the carpet patterns to symbolize the neutrality of Turkmenistan.

TUVALU (too-VAH-loo): Nine small Pacific islands form Tuvalu, a country whose name translates as "nine islands." The stars on the national flag refer not only to the individual islands but also to their positions relative to each other, with "north" at the hoist of the flag. The Union Jack refers to links with the country's former colonial master, Great Britain. The national flag was first hoisted on Independence Day, October 1, 1978; the designer of the flag was Vione Natano. A different flag was used from October 1995 until April 1997, in which the Union Jack was omitted but the national coat of arms and two red stripes were added.

UGANDA (oo-GAN-duh): On October 9, 1962, Uganda, formerly a British colony, became an independent country under the national flag that it continues to use. The black-yellow-red stripes originally were found in the flag of the Uganda People's Congress, which won the elections just prior to independence. National flag colors in many other countries are also based on those of dominant local political parties. The Uganda colors stand for the people, sunshine, and brotherhood. In the center of the flag on a white disk is a crested crane, long recognized as the national bird.

UKRAINE (yoo-KRANE): In the revolutionary year of 1848 many people rallied in support of self-government for Ukraine. As their symbol, they chose the colors found in the coat of arms used by the city of Lviv, a blue shield with a yellow lion. After World War I, Ukrainians briefly gained national independence. In 1918–1921, they used a flag with stripes of yellow over blue, later changed to blue over yellow. That design was revived on January 28, 1992, after Ukraine again became an independent country. The yellow stands for Ukraine's fields of wheat, and blue for the skies over them.

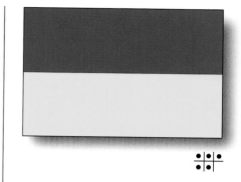

UNITED ARAB EMIRATES (yoo-NIE-tud AHR-ub EH-muh-rates): For a century there were many small Arab emirates (states ruled by emirs) under British protection along the southern coast of the Arabian Gulf. The states eventually decided to unite, and on December 2, 1971, they achieved independence as the United Arab Emirates. For their national flag the four pan-Arab colors (see *Kuwait*), used by many other Arab states, were chosen.

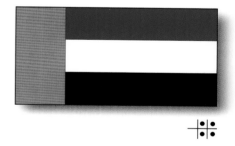

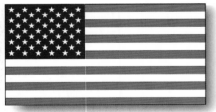

UNITED KINGDOM (yoo-NIE-tud KING-dum): One of the best-known and most widely used flags in the world, the Union Jack (or Union Flag) dates from January 1, 1801. It is a combination of the Cross of St. Andrew of Scotland, dating from the fourteenth century, and the Cross of Saint George, representing England, already displayed in the thirteenth century. They had first been combined in 1606; the saltire (diagonal cross) of Saint Patrick of Ireland was added in 1801. Strictly speaking, the Union Jack is only for use on government and military buildings, although it is widely displayed today by the British people.

UNITED STATES (yoo-NIE-tud states): The fifty-star American flag became official on July 4, 1960, when Hawaii became a state. There had been twenty-six earlier versions with different numbers of stars, symbolizing the states at the time. The first national flag, the Continental Colors, had the British Union Jack in the canton; it was used from 1775 until the first Stars and Stripes was adopted on June 14, 1777. The number of stars and stripes increased to fifteen in 1795 when two new states joined. A new law was adopted in 1818, reducing the stripes to thirteen for each of the original colonies and having the stars correspond to the number of states. The colors—derived from British flags—have no official symbolism.

URUGUAY (OOR-uh-gwie): Revolution against Spanish rule in the southern part of South America began in Argentina. The flag chosen—of blue-white-blue horizontal stripes—came to represent liberty throughout the region, including Uruguay, then known as the Eastern Strip. The nine blue and white stripes in the flag of Uruguay refer to the departments into which the country was originally divided. In the canton of the flag is a golden sun symbolic of independence. The current flag was officially adopted on July 11, 1830, although similar designs had already been used during the previous fifteen years.

UZBEKISTAN (ooz-beh-kih-STAN): The Republic of Uzbekistan has a crescent on its flag to symbolize independence, although it is also a symbol of Islam, the majority religion. The twelve stars stand for the months of the year and the periods of the zodiac. The flag was adopted on November 18, 1991, following independence after the breakup of the Soviet Union. The green stripe is for new life and nature, the white for peace, the red for humanity, and the blue for water and nighttime. The same colors, with different symbolism, had appeared in the last flag of Uzbekistan under Soviet rule.

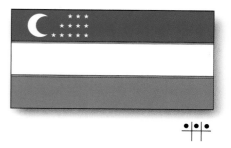

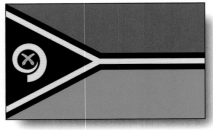

VANUATU (van-oo-AH-too): Near the hoist of the flag is the curved tusk of a pig, considered a religious symbol in Vanuatu. There are also two branches of *namele* (a type of local plant). Both the rich soil of the islands and the Vanuatu people are represented by the black, while green is for agriculture and red is for blood sacrifice. The yellow pall (Y-shape) refers to the position of the islands in the Pacific. The yellow color symbolizes the spread of Christianity, as well as peace. The flag was introduced at the time of Vanuatu independence on July 30, 1980. Similar flags had been proposed for the country earlier.

VATICAN CITY (VAH-tih-kun): The colors yellow and white were chosen by Pope Pius VII early in the nineteenth century to represent his domains. Formerly, the flag of all the popes had been red with two crossed yellow keys. When Vatican City was created on June 8, 1929, as an independent state, the new official flag consisted of yellow and white vertical stripes. The coat of arms on the white stripe has the two traditional keys to symbolize the power of the popes in both spiritual and temporal matters. Above is the traditional tiara worn by the pope on official occasions.

VENEZUELA (veh-nuh-ZWAY-luh): Francisco de Miranda is credited with designing the original national flag of Venezuela. Its yellow stripe stands for the gold of the New World, and the red is for Spain, the two being separated by the blue of the Atlantic Ocean. Different versions of the tricolor were used in the nineteenth century, when Venezuela was united with Colombia and Ecuador. The present flag was adopted on July 15, 1930, when the seven stars, which represent the seven provinces that originally formed the nation, were set in an arc instead of the ring used previously.

VIETNAM (vee-et-NAHM): In 1940, Communist forces in Vietnam fighting the Japanese adopted a red flag with a yellow star. In 1945 the same design was used when they proclaimed the Democratic Republic of Vietnam. In 1955 that flag was slightly modified. After years of struggle against the French, the Americans, and political opponents, the Communists, unified the entire country under that flag on July 2, 1976. The five points of the star stand for the social classes in the country—workers, peasants, military, intellectuals, and people who own small businesses. Use of the color red and a star are typical of Communist governments.

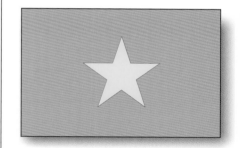

101

YEMEN (YEH-mun): In 1962 a revolution in the northern part of Yemen introduced the Arab Liberation Flag with its horizontal red-white-black stripes, plus a green star in the center. In 1967 the same stripes were used by forces in the south that overthrew British rule in their land. When they proclaimed independence for South Yemen, a blue triangle with a red star was added to their flag. The two Yemens united on May 22, 1990, under a simple tricolor of red (symbolizing the blood shed for freedom and unity), white (for a bright future), and black (for the dark days of the nation's past).

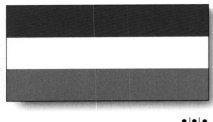

YUGOSLAVIA (yoo-goe-SLAH-vee-uh): The three Slavic colors were first chosen by Russia's Czar Peter the Great in 1699. Following World War I, several Slavic nations in southeastern Europe united to form Yugoslavia. Their common colors were adapted to create the new Yugoslav flag of blue-white-red horizontal stripes. Under the Communist regime of 1946–1991, a red star was added in the center of the same flag. The flag first adopted in 1918 is still in use, although the Communist star was omitted on April 27, 1992. In March 2002 it was announced that the name of the country was being changed to *Serbia and Montenegro*, the two republics that make up the country.

ZAMBIA (ZAM-bee-uh): The United National Independence Party (UNIP) led the country then known as Northern Rhodesia to independence as the Republic of Zambia on October 24, 1964. The colors of the UNIP flag were introduced in the new national flag hoisted at that time. Green is for agriculture, and the eagle symbolizes both freedom and the overcoming of national difficulties. The stripes are for the independence struggle (red), for the African people (black), and for the chief resource of Zambia, copper (orange). The flag design is unusual in having its symbols positioned at the fly end.

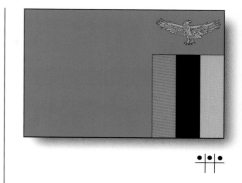

ZIMBABWE (zim-BAH-bway): The country formerly known as Southern Rhodesia (or Rhodesia) was populated by an African majority that had little say in the government. After the dominant white government was defeated in free elections, independence was proclaimed for the Republic of Zimbabwe on April 18, 1980. Its new flag bore the distinctive "Zimbabwe bird," created centuries ago by a local civilization. The flag colors were for the people (black), the liberation struggle (red), agriculture (green), mineral wealth (yellow), and peace and progress (white). The red star was included in the flag to symbolize the commitment to socialism. The red, green, and yellow come from the pan-African colors (see *Mali*).

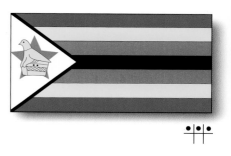

103

NATIONS GROUPED BY CONTINENT

AFRICA

Algeria
Angola
Benin
Botswana
Burkina Faso
Burundi
Cameroon
Cape Verde
Central African
  Republic
Chad
Comoros
Congo, Republic of
Congo, Democratic
  Republic of the
Côte d'Ivoire
Djibouti
Egypt
Equatorial Guinea
Eritrea
Ethiopia
Gabon
Gambia, The
Ghana
Guinea
Guinea-Bissau
Kenya
Lesotho
Liberia
Libya
Madagascar
Malawi
Mali
Mauritania
Mauritius
Morocco
Mozambique
Namibia
Niger
Nigeria
Rwanda
São Tomé and
  Príncipe
Senegal
Seychelles
Sierra Leone
Somalia
South Africa
Sudan
Swaziland
Tanzania
Togo
Tunisia
Uganda
Zambia
Zimbabwe

ASIA

Afghanistan
Armenia
Azerbaijan
Bahrain
Bangladesh
Bhutan
Brunei
Cambodia
China
Cyprus
Georgia
India
Indonesia
Iran
Iraq
Israel
Japan
Jordan
Kazakhstan
Korea, North
Korea, South
Kuwait
Kyrgyzstan
Laos
Lebanon
Malaysia
Maldives
Mongolia
Myanmar
Nepal
Oman
Pakistan
Philippines
Qatar
Saudi Arabia
Singapore
Sri Lanka
Syria
Taiwan
Tajikistan
Thailand
Turkmenistan
United Arab
  Emirates
Uzbekistan
Vietnam
Yemen

AUSTRALASIA

Australia
Fiji
Kiribati
Marshall Islands
Micronesia
Nauru

New Zealand
Palau
Papua New Guinea
Samoa
Solomon Islands
Tonga
Tuvalu
Vanuatu

EUROPE
Albania
Andorra
Austria
Belarus
Belgium
Bosnia-Herzegovina
Bulgaria
Croatia
Czech Republic
Denmark
Estonia
Finland
France
Germany
Greece
Hungary
Iceland
Ireland
Italy
Latvia
Liechtenstein
Lithuania
Luxembourg
Macedonia
Malta
Moldova
Monaco
Netherlands

Norway
Poland
Portugal
Romania
Russia
San Marino
Slovakia
Slovenia
Spain
Sweden
Switzerland
Turkey
Ukraine
United Kingdom
Vatican City
Yugoslavia

NORTH AMERICA
Antigua and Barbuda
Bahamas
Barbados
Belize
Canada
Costa Rica
Cuba
Dominica
Dominican Republic
El Salvador
Grenada
Guatemala
Haiti
Honduras
Jamaica
Mexico
Nicaragua
Panama
St. Kitts and Nevis
St. Lucia

St. Vincent and
    the Grenadines
Trinidad and
    Tobago
United States

SOUTH AMERICA
Argentina
Bolivia
Brazil
Chile
Colombia
Ecuador
Guyana
Paraguay
Peru
Suriname
Uruguay
Venezuela

FLAG-RELATED TERMS

apartheid: a system that segregates races and gives them different political rights and power (for example, South Africa until 1994)

bicolor: a flag consisting of two stripes, usually vertical or horizontal, each with a different color

canton: a rectangular area in the upper hoist corner of a flag that bears a special design

coat of arms: a design, usually including a shield, that provides a standard arrangement of symbols recognized as standing for a country, province, corporation, etc.

cockade: a badge made of ribbon and worn to express a political point of view

crescent: a symbol in the shape of a new moon, often used to stand for the Islamic religion

emblem: a graphic design used as part of a flag or coat of arms

ensign: the national flag of a ship

field: the background of a flag

fimbriation: a very narrow border to an emblem or symbol

fly: the outer end or edge of a flag

hoist (*noun*): the end or edge of a flag normally attached to a pole or rope

hoist (*verb*): to raise a flag on a pole

motto: words or sayings used as a symbol for a nation, province, corporation, etc.

Nordic: referring to certain northern countries of Europe (Iceland, Norway, Sweden, Denmark, Finland)

obverse: the front side of a flag, normally seen when the pole is to the observer's left

pall: a Y-shaped figure used as a symbol

pan-African: including many or all parts of Africa

pan-Arab: including many or all parts of Arab-populated countries

saber: a sword used in battle

saltire: a diagonal cross used as a symbol

secede: to withdraw from a larger territory (for example, Bangladesh seceded from Pakistan in 1971)

Shield of David: a six-pointed symbol used by Israel and by Jews, often mistakenly called the Star of David

symbolism: the meaning given to an object, action, or design; also, the use of objects and designs to convey special meanings

tribar/triband: a flag consisting of three stripes, usually vertical or horizontal, with two different colors

tricolor: a flag consisting of three stripes, usually vertical or horizontal, each with a different color

trident: a spear with three prongs

Union Jack: a flag that combines symbols of several areas; especially, any version of the Union Flag of Great Britain

United Nations: an organization founded in 1945 to promote peace and other world improvements, currently consisting of 189 independent countries

vexillology: the study of all aspects of flags

FOR FURTHER INFORMATION

There are many magazines, books, Web sites, and other sources of information on flags. Here are some of the best places to learn more about vexillology:

Magazine

The Flag Bulletin, published bimonthly by Flag Research Center, Winchester, Massachusetts 01890

Books

Crampton, William. *The World of Flags*. Skokie, Ill.: Rand McNally, 1998.

Ryan, Siobhán. *Flags of the World*. New York: Dorling Kindersley, 1999.

Smith, Whitney. *Flags Through the Ages and Across the World*. New York: McGraw-Hill, 1975.

Znamierowski, Alfred. T*he World Encyclopedia of Flags*. London: Anness, 1999.

Web Sites

The Flag Research Center
http://www.vexillology.com
This site offers content and graphics from the world's biggest flag library, the online edition of the world's largest circulation flag magazine, biographies of "flag people," hints on avoiding unreliable flag sources, and flags from all countries, past and present.

North American Vexillological Association
http://www.nava.org
This Web site displays all sorts of information on flags, including articles, events, recommended books, volunteer and membership information, flags of Native Americans, nautical flags, a dictionary of vexillology, and even a page for kids.